REDISCOVERING
KAI
A Journey to Hope,
Fortitude and
Second Chances

REDISCOVERING KAI

A Journey to Hope, Fortitude and Second Chances

Based on a True Story

Hezekiah L. Montgomery

REDISCOVERING KAI

Copyright © 2013 by Hezekiah L. Montgomery

All rights reserved.

ISBN: 978-0-9996176-0-1

AUTHOR'S NOTE

This book is based on a true story. I have tried to recreate events, locales, and conversations from my memories of them. In order to maintain their anonymity, in some instances I have changed the names of individuals and places. I may have changed some identifying characteristics and details, such as physical properties, occupations, and places of residence, and used artistic license.

The main character, Kai, got caught up in something that was very foreign to him, and once he tasted it, he didn't want to give it up. Kai had the world in his hands at one time, but due to family circumstances his whole world started to change, little by little, and he never even suspected that he'd end up in a situation later in life that would turn his world literally upside down.

Many people that get caught up in his kind of situation normally would give up, but not Kai. He has his mother's fortitude and she was a woman that never quit, no matter what. As Kai was growing up you could basically see that in him. People around him saw it, but he didn't; he thought it was something that he created. No, it was something that was inherited from a woman that loved him, but she couldn't give him the things he needed to prepare him for life or for what was ahead of him. The only thing she could do was love him and be there when she could.

When we first accept Christ into our hearts we think that's the end of it. No, there's more than that. We have to nurture that relationship, and Kai didn't. He accepted Christ into his heart at a very young age and thought that was the end of it. He, like all young people, thought he knew everything. He read his Bible and knew plenty of verses, but that was just intellect. He wasn't saturated with it to keep him safe from the snares Satan was going to set for him as he was getting older. He was the man, everyone looked to him because he was almost the perfect Christian, but he had an enemy that's very relentless and patient and was just waiting for the perfect opportunity to attack, and that's just what he did. He attacked Kai, and Kai never knew what hit him, it just came!

ACKNOWLEDGMENTS

I would give thanks and praise to God and those who helped with the book. This book would have never happened if it wasn't for the real friends that God has placed in my life, and I truly thank Him every day for them. I'd first like to thank my best friends in Philadelphia, Pennsylvania. I love you guys, and I pray for God's blessings on you and your family daily. I'd also like to thank my best friend here in Baltimore, Maryland, Ms. Tina. Thank you for believing in me when others didn't. I know it may have been rough, but you never gave up hope in me, and the Lord used you to nurture me spiritually. Your prayers didn't go unanswered, they were truly heard.

I'd like to thank my family in Philadelphia as well. I know I've been missing in action for more than twenty years, but you never stopped loving me and that love has kept me the past few years of my life. I've learned that family is important. When things happen to us, family will always be there, and you've been there for me from the beginning till now. Just know that this won't be the only book I write. From talking to several family members, this is just the beginning of what God is going to use to help all of us as we're moving to the next level of our lives.

The past twenty-four years of my life have been a process to get me to where I am now, and I thank God for using every one of you, every situation, and every heartache to move me to what I am in Him today. I'm at peace with myself, and only God can give you that kind of peace.

I'd like to thank my therapist, Dr. Stevenson Cash, for everything he did as well. He used the gift that God gave him to give me a new outlook on life. Not every therapist can use the world's wisdom in a situation and also apply God's word and prayer to it, but he did, and I'm truly grateful to him for that. The funny thing is that when I would call him to check up on him or with questions, he would still ask if I was OK, and that, too, is appreciated; that someone would have that much concern for me, to make sure I'm going to make it in life. Dr. Cash, you were truly an angel in disguise.

And lastly, if there's anyone I've forgotten, please forgive me, it's not intentional. This book has been a three-year process, and we know that we can't remember everything that's gone on for the past three years of our lives, but we can get close. So if I've forgotten anyone, please pardon me and enjoy *Rediscovering Kai*.

Oh, yeah, don't let me forget: thank you, McDonald's and Panera Bread, for letting me use your Wi-Fi as I sat many a night with a cup of coffee and typed away. You too are greatly appreciated.

DEDICATION

I would like to dedicate this book to people that I want to help or that will receive help and encouragement from this story. I dedicate it to those out there who are going through something, that are felons, have a criminal record, etc., so they will know not to give up and that there is hope. You too can go from tribulation to triumph and a second chance.

Also, I would like to thank my church family for being real men and women of God. Real praying, Holy Ghost-sanctified people of God. God used you to nurture me, bring me back to Him and keep me there. All your prayers have kept me going through every tear, every hurt, and every circumstance, and I thank you. I will truly be indebted to you.

And a special dedication to Dr. Stevenson Cash: you lost your battle with cancer, but you're at peace now, you're home with your Heavenly Father looking down on us. You are truly missed and will be remembered forever. God used you to help me get back to where I needed to be. I want you to know that you've been an influence in my life since you started working with me, and you helped me understand how I got into my situation and how to stay out of it. Thank you for always praying with me after every session. Again, you were an angel in disguise, and I thank you.

And my final dedication is to my sweet little Cricket: you're grown up now, and I know God is with you. You're a young lady, driving, working, and making a mark on the world. You've inspired me to continue on, because I know deep down inside that you knew I'd make it, regardless of what the circumstances are. Thank you for forgiving me and giving me another chance on life. God used you in a mighty way to change me into the man I am and to understand my calling from Him. So please have a blessed life and stay as sweet as you are.

CONTENTS

Preface 1

Chapter One: Meet Kai 3

Chapter Two: Running 5

Chapter Three: Sexual Immorality 11

Poem: My Destiny 16

Chapter Four: Internet Whore 17

Chapter Five: The Fall 23

Chapter Six: The More Hands 29

Chapter Seven: The Pastor 33

Chapter Eight: The Board 37

Chapter Nine: Myron 41

Poem: Missed 45

Chapter Ten: Bail 47

Chapter Eleven: The Glass 51

Chapter Twelve: Just Like Judas 55

Chapter Thirteen: Bible Studies 57

Chapter Fourteen: Young Timothy 59

Chapter Fifteen: Two Brothers 63

Chapter Sixteen: Eighty-Six Days of Intimacy 67

Chapter Seventeen: The Covenant 73

Poem: So Don't Throw Away Your Bold Faith 76

Chapter Eighteen: The Registration 79

Chapter Nineteen: Transitional Help 83

Chapter Twenty: The Hill 89

Chapter Twenty-One: The Therapy 91

Chapter Twenty-Two: Thoughts 95

Chapter Twenty-Three: The Good Samaritan 97

Chapter Twenty-Four: Three Years and Eighty-Six Days .. 103

Chapter Twenty-Five: Orphan 107

Chapter Twenty-Six: The Mud 109

Chapter Twenty-Seven: Samantha James,
the Friend Who Found Me 111

Chapter Twenty-Eight: Every Which Way but Right 115

Chapter Twenty-Nine: The Anonymous Call 119

Chapter Thirty: Jacqueline, the Friend 123

Poem: Stay the Course 127

Chapter Thirty-One: The Ex-Husband, the Affair 129

Chapter Thirty-Two: 'Tis Better to Have Loved and
Lost Than Never to Have Loved at All 137

Chapter Thirty-Three: The Divorce 145

Chapter Thirty-Four: Reflection of Marriage 147

Chapter Thirty-Five: Forgiving Myself 153

Chapter Thirty-Six: A Letter to My Mother 155

Chapter Thirty-Seven: Abandoned 161

Chapter Thirty-Eight: The Filter 163

Chapter Thirty-Nine: The Two Hardest
Trials in My Life 165

Chapter Forty: Letter to Cricket 169

Chapter Forty-One: Probation Ending 173

Chapter Forty-Two: Obedience Is Better Than Sacrifice 175

Chapter Forty-Three: Be Not Conformed 179

Chapter Forty-Four: Sifted as Wheat, Luke 22:31–32 183

Epilogue: Letter to Mr. Montgomery 185

For if anyone is a hearer of the word and not a doer, he is like a man observing his natural face in a mirror; For he observes himself, goes away, and immediately forgets what kind of man he was. But he who looks into the perfect law of liberty and continues in it, and is not a forgetful hearer but a doer of the work, this one will be blessed in what he does.

—James 1:23–25 (New King James Version)

PREFACE

When I decided to write this story, I had second and third thoughts about it, but I know that was only my fear at work. The word says: "For God hath not given us the spirit of fear; but of power, and of love, and of a sound mind" (2 Timothy 1:7, King James Version). I was worried about what people would think of me. I was worried about my future. But God, who is my Creator and Heavenly Father, said, "Kai, write the story so that people will see that there is hope beyond the pain." You see, we don't ever want to get into a dark place in our lives, but if we do, we need to remember that the light is just a little ahead.

As I'm writing this, I don't want people to get hooked on the heinous crime I committed, but to know that my story didn't stop there. Just as Joseph told his brothers what they meant for harm, the Creator meant for good, when they sold him into slavery and the Heavenly Father in time made him head of Egypt, so that in return he could save his family and his brothers, too (Genesis 45). So the Heavenly Father can take the most messed-up situation and make good come out of it. I believe this because that is what happened to me. The Creator took my messed-up situation and made it turn out not only to bring me back to Him, but to glorify Him, too.

The main problem with society is that it looks at the act and not at all the persons involved. But my Father used this to teach me how to love even when I didn't love myself; how to love even when others didn't love me back. He taught me how not to give up even though I was tired, alone, and just hungry and thirsty for more of Him in my life. You see, my Father was the only one who could take an awful situation and use it to transform me into the image of His Son, Jesus Christ, so that I could be equipped to carry out His will. He took me and my situation from tribulation to triumph and a second chance.

Chapter One
MEET KAI

I remember a young man that I met many years ago. He was on fire for the Lord. He walked with Him, prayed to Him; he served Him with all his heart. People looked to him and had respect for him. He had a passion to serve the Lord and do His complete will. He wasn't pressured with the bothers of this world; he just wanted to do what was right. He had a passion for music, and children, and wanted to serve his community in any way he could.

That young man's name was Hezekiah, Kai for short. Kai was born in Philadelphia, Pennsylvania, in 1963 to Marie L. Pratt and Hezekiah Montgomery. He had the world in his hands for the first ten years of his life. He went to the St. Augustine Catholic School from kindergarten to eighth grade, and was always taught the Bible and the word of God. He grew up with a passion for reading anything and everything.

In the past fifteen years, he buried a mother and a father; he has seen the death and destruction of not only one marriage but two. He spent eighty-six days in the Baltimore Detention Facility (BDF). His wife abandoned him for her ex-husband, who was also married at the time. He was abandoned by his spiritual leader and his pastor, to lie in jail without any spiritual guidance, even after writing them and asking them for help. He was left in the BDF with just one pair of underwear and socks. He hurt a child he loved dearly; he lost a new car, his apartment, and a good job. He was abandoned and alone. Let me tell you about me.

Chapter Two
RUNNING

A few weeks ago, when I was at work, a couple of friends and I were talking about running. I told them that I knew I could outrun them; as usual, they said they could run faster than me. But I knew I could outrun them because many of them smoke, drink, and are just lazy. I walk all the time, and at times have to run to catch the bus. Then Tasha said something that made me think. She said, "I think Kai can run because he's probably been running all his life." She even quoted the famous line from the movie *Forrest Gump*, "Run, Forrest, run!" After she said that, it hit me: she's right. After the age of ten, when my life took a total spin and changed, I've been running. I've been running to get an education, I've been running to be the perfect Christian, and I've been running to find that person who will love me right.

I started running to get my education after I was forced out of my first home at the age of ten and had to go live with my aunt and cousins. I said to myself that I had to make something of myself so that I could move on and be something different.

Don't get me wrong, I loved my family, but I knew there was something different about me. Along with my cousins, I started taking piano lessons from Ms. Dolly Macon when I was about ten years old. I was very good at it and had an appreciation for it. It was something I'd always wanted to do, so I was doing it, and even that was a struggle when it came to my family. I felt like I was the only one that wanted to do something different. I wanted to learn as much about music as I could from Ms. Macon. My family thought I was crazy because I kept going and kept practicing, song by song, till I learned it.

When I started high school, I wanted to be a doctor, but the school I went to, George Frederick High (GFH), was a trade school, and had music as a major, so you know what I did. I became a music major and learned to play the trumpet. It really wasn't that difficult for me to learn to play it because I had at least five years of music instruction under my belt. GFH was fun; I even joined the choir, and my friends and I had three great years in the music department, exploring and learning more about music.

I still had becoming a doctor in mind, so when I graduated from GFH, I started attending the Community College of Philadelphia, taking classes that would go toward my goal of medicine. But when I hit the math classes my grades started to decline. After my first full year, I made a decision: I decided to transfer to the music department and become a music teacher. The funny thing about it was that I was always hanging around the music department; eventually I auditioned, and then majored in music.

After a couple of years there, I had my graduating recital, which went well till I had to play the andante part of a Mozart sonata and fumbled the ball completely, though I did recover. I probably would have gotten a B for the recital, but ended up with a C because of my memory lapse.

After the recital, I decided it was time to go to a university to continue my music career. I wanted to be a music teacher, and my high school music teacher, Mrs. Trent, was my idol when it came to music. When I got to high school and played the piano for her, I remember to this day that she told me I had played a wrong note. I was playing Bach's Minuet in G. I told her that I hadn't played a wrong note, so we went back and forth for a second, then I looked at the music again—and lo and behold, I was playing a wrong note. That was the moment that caught my attention. I was a perfectionist when it came to my music. She had a genuine concern for me and I didn't see it at that moment. Mrs. Trent asked who I was taking lessons with, and I told her it was Ms. Dolly Macon at my church. She then asked had I ever considered taking more lessons with anyone else. I told her no, because I was dedicated to Ms. Macon and didn't want to leave her.

Mrs. Trent and I went back and forth about this, as if she was my mother, and wanted more for me. I decided to ask Ms. Macon if it would be OK if I pursued another teacher, and she said it was fine, because she had done all she could do with me and wanted me to excel. So with her blessing, I went back to Mrs. Trent and said, "OK, I'll pursue another teacher." She told me about the Philadelphia Music Academy, and gave me the information. I called, went to the one in South Philadelphia and set up lessons, and was on my way to taking private lessons with new instructors. You see, Mrs. Trent had seen talent in me and wanted to help nurture that talent. Did I understand that at first? No, but as time went on, my knowledge of piano music and my repertoire started to grow, and I was gaining a greater appreciation for music.

I then joined the choir, was in band, and was having the greatest time in my life with music. Our band director was the greatest I've ever known. I had actually run into him in junior high, when he was the music director for the first musical I did, *Guys and Dolls*. After junior high I had to pick a high school, so I picked GFH and chose music as my forte. He gave me the trumpet to learn, and since I already knew and read music, learning to play the trumpet was a breeze. So you see why I wanted to be a music teacher. Even though I started college wanting to be a doctor, music was always in my heart and soul. And to be honest, math sucked, and after I found out how much math was involved, music took over.

I then transferred to Temple University as a music education major. I started all my classes as everyone did, had a new teacher as everyone did, and tried to work a full-time job. But as time went on, my work and practice schedules weren't coming together as they should, and I think God saw that. I actually got fired from the job I had at that time, which was managing a McDonald's. I always did my best while working on my degree in music education. I'll be honest, I didn't do well in music history because of my writing skills, but after I took the appropriate classes to bring those up, everything was better.

I learned the hard way that if you don't pay attention to the important classes in high school, it will affect you later in college. When I was at the community college, I struggled with English 101. I struggled so badly that it took me three tries to pass it in order to go on to English 102. But by that time I was transferring to Temple University, and the blessing was that it accepted about fifty of the accredited classes I took at community college.

I did struggle while at the university. I struggled because I was always trying to be the perfect Christian and family guy; when my family needed me, I was there. I was playing the piano for my church, with choir rehearsals to do and programs to prepare for once in a while. So my focus wasn't always where it should have been and I started to go downhill. It got so bad that I was put on academic probation. Now mind you, this wasn't the first time I'd been on academic probation; I was on it while in community college. While on probation I had to bring up my grades in other courses, to prove that I could handle the course load. I was also kicked out of the college of music and had to audition again if I wanted to continue in music education. Well, you know me; I got a teacher, got to practicing again, and then got ready for another audition.

Today, I clearly see that God's favor has been with me throughout my life, because guess who was on the jury when I auditioned to get back into the college of music? The teacher I was taking lessons from. She was the one that prepared me for the audition, and the others saw that I had improved. Only God can have your teacher be there when you're doing your audition to get into a school—only God.

So when I went to talk to one of the professors, Mrs. Clancy, she was shocked, and I remember to this day what she said when I was in her office. She said, "Mr. Montgomery, you are so tenacious." I had to look that up; it generally meant that I wasn't one to let go and give up. And I guess she was right; if there was something I wanted, I've never given up. To this day, I'm still a very tenacious person, and I know it was only God who gave that to me. So you see, I've always been running in my life, like Forrest, and like him, I never gave up.

Chapter Three
SEXUAL IMMORALITY

There is a reason God said that sex is meant for the marriage bed and should not be defiled. Why? Because he knew that we would not be able to handle it if it's not controlled and has boundaries. The boundary that He gave is marriage. The first married couple was Adam and Eve; they were married in God's eyes. "And they were both naked, the man and his wife, and were not ashamed" (Genesis 2:25, KJV). He formed them for each other and Eve was a helpmeet to Adam. "And the LORD God said, it is not good that man should be alone; I will make him a help meet for him" (Genesis 2:18, KJV).

So what did society do? It took what God created to be beautiful and ran with it. That's why in the word it said that man should not fornicate, or have sex outside marriage, because it's against all of God's principles. "Flee fornication. Every sin that a man doeth is without the body; but he that committeth fornication sinneth against his own body" (1 Corinthians 6:18). As a young man, I always tried to meet someone I could go out with, have a good time, and then maybe marry. Well, I was in love with someone at the age of eighteen, but I was too slow for her; she wanted the bad boy, which I could never understand. As the years went by and I was trying to date here and there, I was always the one that wasn't picked. There I was, thinking I was never going to experience sex, not knowing that God was trying to keep me from getting into something that I was going to regret later.

I once heard an evangelist give her testimony on how she was before God put her on lockdown. In her younger years, she was sleeping with this one and that one, and when she would try to get away there was always some residue left. She explained it this way: when a man sleeps with a woman, he's giving her something, and the woman is receiving from him. He's the giver and she's the receiver. So if he had slept with another woman, and then slept with her, whatever spirits were on that other woman would be carried through him to the one he was sleeping with now. And it's the same when reversed: whatever spirits were on the woman, she would give them to the man. What happens is that we start to get soul ties to this man or woman, and we know it's wrong, but we don't want to let them go. And even if we let them go, and think we're over them, if they come around, our knees may buckle because they're there. That means you're not over them. They still have power over you.

What I'm saying is, when I had my first sexual experience with my first wife, I didn't know her. I got caught up in fornication thinking it was love. I got caught up in sexual immorality, which was against all of God's rules. So whatever spirits she had from past experiences were being passed on to me. I didn't have any past experiences because she was my first. It was the first of what Satan thought was going to be a lifetime of misery. Yes, I enjoyed it, I would be a liar if I said I didn't, but the problem was that I was enjoying it the wrong way. And soon the feeling of fun began to change, and what I once thought was right turned out not to be right later on down the road. I thought I was in love, but in fact I was just basically in lust.

Neither one of my wives truly knew me. I didn't get to know them either. Why? Because each was started off the same way—fornication. And when you go against the rules of God, as Paul says: "for the wages of sin is death" (Romans 6:23). Nothing good could have come from it because nothing was done right. We never became friends. So, as one of my best friends said whenever we talked about it, I was basically going through a *Groundhog Day* scenario, hoping to wake up to something new, and not the same thing.

Another problem is that when sex is involved, you're not focused on who that person is but on how it feels to be in the bed with him or her. I never got to know my first wife before we married, even though we dated for two years before the wedding. She had anger management problems, which I never saw until after our wedding day. I found out as we started to have arguments. She would start beating on me and I wouldn't hit her back, because I saw my father beat my mother and I didn't want to be like him. But I got tired of the fights that always started before I went to work in the morning. One day, after four years, I did retaliate, and from that retaliation I ended up spending time in a cell until she, her mom, and my mother came to get me. That was one of the worst moments of my life. I'd never been in jail, and for my mom to have to come get me…I didn't know what to say. I was her baby, and there I was.

My second wife was no different. I didn't even know her a whole year, but the sex was good—yeah, yeah, I know, the same old, same old—and we got married. Now, get this, the divorce from my first wife finally went through about a month prior to me marrying my second wife. Yes, I know that was insane, but I did it. But again, I didn't know her, and only after marrying her did I find out all the things about her that I should have learned prior to marrying her. But the sex was good, we were truly compatible, and my eyes were glazed over. The signs where there and I ignored them, because I was caught up in the sex and fornication. An old girlfriend who loved me dearly as a friend was trying to tell me. Her mom even tried to tell us that it was wrong, but we did it anyway. So again the sex and lust won out, and sexual immorality got another home run due to my ignorance and disobedience to the word of God. If I would have backed up, prayed, stayed in the word, and abstained from fornicating, I'm quite sure I would have gotten another answer. Why? Because there wouldn't have been any kind of soul tie to her. That's the bond that's the hardest to break; your souls are entwined and you yearn for each other when you're apart.

"For this is the will of God, [even] your sanctification, that ye should abstain from fornication: That every one of you should know how to possess his vessel in sanctification and honour; Not in the lust of concupiscence, even as the Gentiles which know not God:" (1 Thessalonians 4:3, KJV).

When sexual immorality is invited into your life, your brain gets foggy and starts forgetting what's right and what's wrong. You can be the smartest man or woman around; you will fall for it all the time. Why? Because you're caught up in what the world says is OK, or you're caught up in your own desires, wants, likes, passion, and pleasures. Even if you're the strongest, like Samson, you will fall for a Delilah. Why? Because Satan's schemes are always different but the same. If you don't stay prayed up, read up, and kept up, you'll fall for it every time. I was a college student and then a college graduate, and as intelligent as I was, I fell for the oldest scheme around. Why? Because I didn't stay prayed up, and Satan knew my weakness.

But if we stay in the word and pray every day, when the enemy comes with his schemes, we'll know what they are and won't fall for his plans like we used to. We have to keep our eyes on our Heavenly Father; once He frees us from sexual immorality, and we get a new role in life, then we'll be able to practice celibacy with no problem. Why? Because we know in our heart that we want to please Him, not him or her.

POEM
MY DESTINY

I know my destiny is under attack,

I know my destiny is going through warfare,

I know that God has a plan for my destiny in Him.

Chapter Four
INTERNET WHORE

I know what you're thinking: what is he talking about now? Well, here it is. In my marriage to my first wife, I thought I knew what I was doing when it came to making love to the woman I was married to. You see, we didn't do it right; we met, started dating, and then started fornicating. This was my first real experience with sex; I'm quite sure it wasn't hers. So as we were having sex, I started experimenting with oral sex and realized that I enjoyed it. I wanted more all the time. We had regular sex as well, but I totally enjoyed oral sex, without a doubt.

I would work all day, go to school, and then end up at her house for the evening. Her room was in the basement of her mother's house, so we'd do what every couple did. Start off kissing, necking, caressing, and then end up having sex. I'd leave early the next morning so no one would know I was there, unless they saw my car parked close to her house. All this time I was thinking that I was pleasing her, but deep down inside her, I wasn't.

So after fornicating, I'm thinking I'm in love with her and want to marry her. My family reunion on my father's side was coming up, so I decided we'd take that long drive down to South Carolina and then I would propose to her in front of my family. We took the drive, which was extremely long, and seemed even longer since I had to do all the driving myself. We finally get there, have dinner with the family, and I propose to her on her birthday. She didn't know what was happening; the ring was in a champagne glass, and as I made the toast to her, she had to really look to see it. When she realized what was going on, she started to cry. Before dinner she was making my life a living hell because she didn't know what was going on. My mom and her mom did, and my family, but not her. So she got her engagement ring that night for her birthday.

We started making wedding plans, got married a couple of years later, and then started our life together. Well, whoever said it was going to be easy from that point on was wrong. When all hell breaks loose it really breaks loose. I didn't know before I married her that when she got angry and we had disagreements I'd be the one getting beat up, knocked upside the head, or even pushed down the stairs. She had an anger management problem I never knew about. So, for the first four years of our marriage I was abused when she would get angry, but I would never tell anyone because I thought if I did, I'd look like a fool. There I was, a man, and I let a woman beat on me. But what kept me from hitting her back was that when I was younger, I saw my father beat on my mother, and she made me promise that I would never hit a woman.

As the years went by I got her everything she wanted—a car, a house, and things to go in it—and she still wasn't satisfied. And to top it off, my mother got sick with cancer, which was a blow to me. It came to the point that my mother needed to come live with us so that I could help take care of her while she was going through her first bout with cancer. My wife didn't want her to come live with us because her dad had stayed with us when we were newlyweds. It was uncomfortable financially, and I honestly asked if her brother and sisters could help out as well. She took that personally, so when I needed to help my mother she made it hard for me.

Now, due to this and other stress I was not pleasing her sexually. I had the stress of the job, the stress of my mom being sick with cancer, and now my wife wasn't being pleased in the bedroom. I started feeling inadequate and couldn't perform the way I wanted to. At that time I didn't know what was going on, but as I'm reflecting, it's making sense to me now. She had me get some books from Dr. Johnson's, the adult store on Thirteenth and Arch, to help me learn how to please her. But it wasn't working, so I started getting really frustrated.

So what did I do? I had just gotten a computer and learned how to get on the Internet. I started chatting on AOL and Black Planet, meeting women online who were single, and I'll be honest—I'd lie and say I was, too. I'd get their phone numbers and call them, or just chat all the time when I didn't have anything to do. When my wife was up in the sewing room that I put together for her, with the sewing machine that I took out a loan to get her, I'd be in my basement office talking to other women. I learned about them, e-mailed them, and sent pictures, and they sent pictures to me. I was more comfortable talking to them than to the woman I was living with. Go figure.

Then it happened. I started wanting to meet them in person because I was living with my wife but still lonely. And on top of that, she would tear me down mentally and physically, which is something a woman should never do, or want to do, to her man.

By this time my mom had gotten over the first bout with cancer and I thought all was well, but it wasn't. In the next couple of years, I was still going to church, still playing the piano for my church, but was getting more and more engrossed in the Internet, not knowing it was getting a hold of my mind. I was telling these young ladies what was going on in my life and they were telling me what was going on in theirs, and relationships began to build. Then it hit me. My mom's cancer came back and I didn't even know it. She was trying to call and tell me, but I wasn't paying attention. I thought everything was fine, and I was trying to live my life. Since things really weren't going well with my wife and me in the bed, I continued to try to meet women online. I was also meeting women at work. It wasn't anything planned, but when someone took an interest in me, she pulled me all the way in. I remember Mrs. Samuels; we were both music teachers and met during a yearly concert with all the kids. We exchanged numbers and it was on. She wasn't happy with her marriage and I wasn't happy with mine, so we basically had an affair here and there, and no one knew but us.

I had an online experience with Fanny McGlaughin. We clicked immediately. She lived in California; her husband was draining her financially because of drugs. I was dealing with my sick mother, who was now about to die, and a messed-up marriage. So we talked, sent pictures, and got to know each other. I don't know if my wife ever found out, but I was really into Fanny.

When my mother started to get worse, I didn't know. To this day, I think she was trying to tell me, but I was so busy and going through so much that I couldn't even hear her. When she died I was distraught. I didn't know what to do. My brother didn't make it to be there when she passed; instead, he ran back to Baltimore due to fear. So I had to take care of the arrangements for the funeral, and find the money to do that. The blessing was that the Lord took care of all that, with money still left for my brother and me. So I saved his half, gave my wife some money to keep her quiet for a minute, and then I did what I wanted with my half. And the one thing I did was send some to Fanny in California to help with a bill and allow her to come see me in Philadelphia for a romantic rendezvous. She came. I got away from home for the weekend and took the bus to the hotel. I don't know what my wife did that weekend, but I think she got suspicious and was looking around for an answer. As always, I tried to hide any evidence of anything that might point her to what I was doing.

When we got to the hotel, it was on. We had a great time, and the sex was off the hook. Fanny knew what was going on at home, and she said, "It's not you, your equipment is working fine, it's her." That was all I needed to hear. I showed her around downtown Philadelphia, we went out to eat and then back to the hotel. She had rented a car, so we had a chance to travel around Philly and see the sights. When the weekend was over, she dropped me off close to home, went back to the hotel, got her things, headed for the airport, and returned to California. Yes, I know it was wrong, and part of me didn't feel good, but I was hurt and needed to find out if it was me.

After that rendezvous there were many more. I caught a plane to Georgia to meet a young lady at a hotel. I met one in a Philly hotel near the airport as well. I was meeting women online like there was nothing more to life. I even drove to Baltimore to meet one who lived past Washington and had family in Philly. By this time I was sleeping on the couch because I didn't want anything to do with my wife. She messed me up mentally and physically, and I didn't want to touch her. Yes, I became an Internet whore. I was still in the church and keeping it all hush-hush. This was the beginning of my end.

Chapter Five
THE FALL

I met my second wife, Keisha, in the summer of 2004. We really hit it off. Even though it was mostly sexual, we decided to get married a year later. Her daughter Cynthia was eleven years old at the time.

During the first year of courting her, her younger children that were with her had a love-hate thing for me. I understood that because I had worked with children my whole life. I could deal with the boy, but what Cynthia was doing I couldn't understand. Until her, I'd never been rejected like that in the beginning. So we had this love-hate thing going on until one day, after she turned twelve, she started slowly liking me. And something weird happened. She started kissing me on the cheek every so often, and once in a while, in a greeting or if leaving, she would kiss me on the lips. Or when we were having a father-daughter evening she would just kiss me. Eventually, before I knew it, one thing led to another, and boom! It got out of hand. To this day, I don't know how it started or got out of hand. I would tell her,

"Hey, this is wrong," and even told her what would happen if it was found out, but it didn't seem she cared. There were times when my wife was going out and I'd tell her to take Cynthia with her, but she didn't want to go.

So that continued, off and on, and even when I wanted to stop it, it would stop for a month and then she'd come back. It would mostly happen when my wife was asleep, because she was on heavy medication. But to skip on, it then evolved into hugging and kissing here and there. I wanted to stop it, but she would always get angry with me. My intellect knew it was wrong, but the silly me who wasn't thinking was more concerned about her feelings. It was discovered one night when Cyndi thought my wife was sleeping. We were petting and my wife came in and found us. At that moment I kind of felt relieved, because I was tired and had never been through anything like that before in my life.

Keisha left the house angry, got my best friend and her best friend—who were sisters and ministers—came back for the children, and left. She then called me the next morning and told me that the pastor had found out, due to her best friend talking to her mother, who's the pastor's wife. He called me and wanted to talk to me that evening. I really didn't have time to talk to him, but he insisted, because I was having a recital at the church that Sunday afternoon and he wasn't going to let the children have the recital until I came to see him. He then sat me down and wanted details; he even taped me because he wanted to protect the church (so he said). It made me feel so humiliated at that time. That whole weekend was a nightmare. At that time I was teaching in an elementary school. My wife was trying to be supportive, so that Monday she went online to find a therapist for me to go to. She found one, Dr. Anthony Bonner. She went with me to see him for six months, trying to figure out how and why it happened. After six months, he told me it was misplaced affection. She didn't know how to show her affection toward me, but she would always tell me that she was jealous of her mother.

But after those six months, my wife left to go live with her mother. She was mad and upset, but we tried to make the marriage work being separated. She had to report it, but didn't report the whole thing because she and Cyndi didn't want anything to happen to me. The church members kept calling DHS, which said the information was found to be unsubstantiated. So as we were trying to still be a family while apart, I tried my best to get it right and stay on track as a husband and stepfather, but didn't have too much help to do that. The church barred me as a musician, I was alone in my apartment many times, I kept trying to help her financially in her escapades, but to no avail. She was still bitter. And when I thought she forgave me, she didn't. The only thing we still had in common was that the sex was good. She eventually told me that she only married me because the sex was good. I told her that she didn't have to do that, but she did.

It was discovered at the end of December 2006. I went to counseling from January to June 2007, and that's when she left. Well, a few years later, in the summer of 2008, I was offered an application to be a 911 operator for the police department. I wanted to make more money, so I filled it out. A year later they called for the background check, and then all hell broke loose. They did the preliminary polygraph questions, and when asked if I had ever been accused of anything with children, I told them about what happened, and even told them that the family had tried counseling. They didn't hear anything except that I did something with a child. They reopened the case, and several months later, in September 2009, they had a warrant for my arrest. My wife was upset at the time, but I turned myself in, thinking that she would be there to help me. She hired a lawyer, who was going to get me out with no conviction. For some reason, Cyndi, after all these years, having never said anything to the three professional doctors and therapist she saw, told her dad. Mind you, my wife had told me that he was accused of doing something inappropriate to her as well, when she was smaller. But anyway, I was amazed. After it was found out, I took her all over Baltimore to get help, and even wanted to get my wife help, but neither wanted to talk.

So, as I was thinking that I was going to get bailed out, something happened. Cyndi's real dad stepped in like a knight in shining armor, and helped the family, and did everything for her to help her through this. I didn't know that he was cheating on his wife by having an affair with my wife, in front of the children. To make this long story short, when I thought she was out there trying to help me, she was with him, and he was filling her head with lies to get him off child support of sixteen thousand dollars. She eventually got me out on December 17, 2009, with a plea bargain, which the attorney didn't like. She told the DA to talk to Cynthia, and Cynthia said that I didn't belong in there—that I needed help. Cynthia didn't know that

I'd seen two therapists already and was working on me. But they got me out and put me on the registry. I wanted to get out on bail so that I could at least fight what was going on, but I couldn't do anything but take what was given to me after eighty-six days. I lost my home, my car, everything. She did save some of my things in storage, but again I lost it all.

But the good thing was that while I was in there I got my calling from the Lord to preach. I was forced to leave the church, since Cynthia was also a member. A captain at BDF was an elder there and he knew all about it, and knew that I couldn't be near her. My wife had made an agreement with the DA, but the church didn't accept that, so I was forced out into the cold the first Sunday after getting out. I was finally able to go to church after three months or so, walking up the hill on Old Frederick Road to the church where I am now. I'm a new man and they have accepted me. Even knowing about my background, they still chose to love me. I'm in the Bible institute at my new church, passed the first class with a 4.0 average, and am now carrying a 4.0 in the second class.

My wife still tried to have sex with me until, in April 2010, I found out the whole truth of what had been going on. I made her tell me the truth and she did; she told me about the affair. I decided that I couldn't go on with that soap opera. I was already dealing with what had happened and being on the registry, and she wanted me to accept her being in love with another man. So I chose to get a divorce. I know I hurt Cynthia, but I couldn't take that. I had my first anxiety attack in April 2010, because of him and her; I decided it was too much. She didn't think I was going to do it, and my therapist, Dr. Cash, didn't think so either, but I said life was too short to deal with all this. I'd been married twice already, and knew it was my fault because I put sex first and never became friends. I said I wouldn't do that again.

But I've been blessed. I told the story to friends from home in Philadelphia, and they said, "It's OK, we knew you before all this foolishness happened," and they chose to still love me. I needed that. And my family at home loves me as well. I needed to be surrounded by love and not the foolishness that my wife kept giving me. When I thought she had forgiven me, he came in and did something that turned it all around. I told her, "God forgave me, it's between you and God now." I chose to live right because I made a promise to Him to get it right and to serve Him. Dr. Stephenson Cash has always backed me up, and he did ask the question therapists ask. He said science says that once you're a sex offender there is no change. I told him that God had changed me and healed me a long time ago, when I was in BDF. I got my sanctification, purification, and calling. I did ask him and Dr. Bonner, "Why did Cynthia choose me?" They both said, "Because you were available." Go figure. I'd never hurt any child in my life. And now, because of other offenders out there, instead of being on the registry for ten years, they've made it worse for first timers: it is a lifetime contract. But then there's God.

Chapter Six
THE MORE HANDS

The statement was made the other day: "The more people that put their hands in things, the worse it gets." It wasn't the first time I had heard it, just confirmation that it is true. When it was first discovered by the church that something was going on between my stepdaughter and me, the officials of the church didn't handle it correctly. I'm now in a new church, and it's fascinating to me, when I reflect on the incident, that when saints fall, you are to restore them privately and not make them ashamed of what happened to them all the time. The problem at the moment is the people in the church today are worse than the people in the world. They like to take things in their hands, and they feel the need to help God out. Or they feel that He's taking too long, so they need to pitch in.

We have to get out of the habit of thinking that God needs our help. When we see someone fall, it's not our time to see what we can do to fix it. It's our time to pray for them and ask what we can do to help, if possible. They didn't do that. They started calling here and there, and gossiping, and the more they gossiped, the more the story wasn't straight. The more it wasn't straight, the worse it got.

As Christians, when we see someone in offense and they fall, it's our duty to pray that God will have mercy on them. They didn't have mercy on me. All the emotions arose and I was alone. My wife was already gone; I was home alone, with no one to talk to, and no one to pray for me. I was humiliated for what I did to a child, and didn't know what to do. I did my best day by day to make it.

I had no one that wanted to show me the love of Christ and love me for me. If I wasn't part of a clique, or a family, or in a group, I wasn't important. That's the worst feeling anyone can have. When you go to church, you're alone; when you're home, you're alone; when you're driving and wanting to talk to someone, you're alone. Why? Because again, the more people talk, gossip, and not look toward God, the worse it gets.

What I'm talking about is that I was in a church, but I didn't feel the love of God there. Both my parents died years ago, and my best friend got married, which was a great thing because I couldn't run to her with my problems like I used to. It seemed that when my mother-in-law, the evangelist, came to the church, she was more important than I was. Somewhere down the line it was forgotten that I had been at the church first. I got there in the summer of 2001 and was there until all this craziness came about. But it seemed that my loyalty and dedication weren't appreciated in my time of need. Just remember, it's not always good to want to know what's going on and want to try to put your hands in it to make it come out right. Too many hands will mess up the whole thing, and without God truly being the center of it, it will be to no avail.

Chapter Seven
THE PASTOR

The weekend it was discovered that there was something going on between me and my stepdaughter was also the weekend that I was having a Musical Extravaganza. After my wife went with my best friend and her best friend to her mother's house she texted me the next day. You see, I also had an engagement to play at a Christmas party that Saturday evening, and I think even though she was upset, she still wanted everything that was planned for that weekend to happen. But Satan was busy. She had texted me to tell me that the pastor had found out. I asked her how he had found out. She said that her best friend, Minister Cary, was talking to her mother, Minister Franchise, who was the pastor's wife, on the phone. When Minister Franchise was finished on the phone, the pastor, her husband, asked what they were talking about, and she told him. Now mind you, my wife had asked Minister Cary not to tell anyone, but she was never good at keeping things to herself. Anyway, there we were—the pastor now knew.

The pastor then proceeded to tell my wife to tell me to contact him. I did, and he said that he wanted to see me. I tried to tell him that I had a lot of things on my plate that day and I was getting ready for the recital. Well, he wasn't listening. He wanted me to make arrangements to come over to his house to talk to him about what had happened.

So this was what happened that Saturday evening of December 17, 2006, at his house. When I got there, he and his wife took me to a room where I could talk to them. He got a small tape recorder and wanted to actually tape a confession from me about what had happened. By this time, I was already humiliated about what had happened and needed a pastor myself. He told me that he was taping what I said to cover the church, in case it became public. I didn't want to tell him, but he said if I didn't, he wouldn't let the students play in the program that Sunday afternoon. So I hesitantly told him what had happened and he taped it. To this day, I don't know what he did with that tape. But the main thing was that I felt really humiliated as I was telling my pastor what I had done to hurt a child that I was supposed to have protected. It didn't seem as though he was even worried about me or how I felt about my transgression; he was more concerned about making sure the church didn't get hurt. One thing I've preached my whole Christian life is that the place you go to for services or worship is just a building; it is the people that make up the church, not the building. So, as he was getting his tape recorder ready, I didn't really know what to say. He wanted me to spill my guts and tell him everything, almost in detail, which told me that he wasn't concerned about me. He was more concerned that the church not be liable for anything that came out of this, in case the information was leaked to the public.

You see, that pastor wasn't acting out of mercy for me. He was acting on impulse, he was acting off emotions, and he only wanted to protect the church. I know now that he didn't really care about me; he didn't even know me. I was just his musician that made him look good. I was pimped, and I say this because if you had known me when this happened, you would know I'm not that type of person. You would have known that I must have gotten caught up in something, and needed much prayer and direction to get back to where I needed to be. But, as I said, he didn't know me. He just knew what he had heard. He never took the time to get to know me for me. So when something of this nature happened, he didn't have anything to work with. But again, that's no excuse. When you're a minister, a pastor, you're supposed to take care of the flock, and he didn't. He left me out for the wolves to devour.

I was coerced into telling him because he wasn't going to let the children perform that Sunday if I didn't. People were trying to tell him not to let the kids suffer because of this. I was working hard to make something happen and the devil was just setting the stage to humiliate me. I don't remember everything I told him, but to this day I know how I felt after I left his home. I knew that I had to finish my day, I had a party to do that evening, and I had to get books put together for the program. A lot was happening in that one weekend, and the devil was pulling the strings and setting me up big-time.

My stepdaughter was preparing to play in the program. So you see, in the past forty-eight hours what had happened was discovered, I had talked to the pastor, and then we had to go on that day as if nothing had happened. She was under a lot of pressure, I was under a lot of pressure, my wife was under a lot of pressure, and my mother-in-law was under a lot of pressure. The devil was having a field day with this. He wanted lives destroyed, he wanted a family broken up, he wanted a child destroyed by someone who was supposed to have loved her and protected her. But God was still there, protecting her, me, and all the others.

Chapter Eight

THE BOARD

A few days after what I had done to my stepdaughter was discovered, I was called to a board meeting at the church. They also asked my wife to attend. She sat behind me, the board was in back of her, and the chairman of the board was sitting in front of me, along with the elder of the church. He asked me to reveal my transgression to the board and explain it to them in detail. My best friend, Tina, who was the pastor's daughter, was sitting behind me, along with my wife, Keisha. She wanted to say something but couldn't because the chairman didn't let her. My wife also wanted to say something, but again, the chairman wouldn't let her. He was in total control and wanted me to reveal what I had done.

I looked at him in shame, and also like he was crazy. I was already ashamed of what I'd done and how it was discovered, and now he wanted me to tell a bunch of nosy board members so they would be looking at me in a whole different light. I sat there quietly for a moment, not saying a word, before I told him that I wasn't telling them anything. They didn't know me, and I truly didn't know or trust them. He thought I was about to tell them the whole story and they could pass judgment on me. Well, he thought wrong. So I kept quiet. He wasn't pleased with that. He told me that he was going to have to suggest to the pastor that I be barred from playing, if I wasn't going to tell them. I chose the latter, not to play for that church any longer.

I was truly upset by now, you see. I had already been over to the pastor's house the night after it happened, to explain it to him. So why was I in front of this group of people to repeat the same thing all over again? That was truly ludicrous to me!

I didn't want to talk to the board. I was already on tape; now they wanted me to talk to this group of people who really didn't know me, and all they wanted was gossip. They wouldn't try to help me; they'd try to send me up the river and forget me. At that moment in my life, I didn't trust anyone, because I didn't have anyone I could trust. I didn't feel that I was loved. I felt like I was in a circus and was the featured act. That was one of the worst feelings in my entire life. I felt like I was put on display because I wasn't perfect and I fell. There wasn't anyone to really console me and help me back into the fold. I pray that no one else ever has to go through that.

The problem with the way it was handled was that anyone could have been in my situation and done the same thing. I thank God today for the strength to make it through, even though the so-called "powers that be" didn't do their job. You see, what if I had been someone who couldn't handle the pressure of the meeting with the board, and had woken up the next morning and decided to commit suicide? Then what? I could have done it after I got home from the meeting, because it was too much pressure to meet with them, try to disclose what had happened, and keep my sanity about the whole thing. We have to be very careful when we handle delicate situations like this. Not everyone can handle being treated the way we think they should be treated in some situations. If we don't do it with loving, caring, and being full of mercy, we too may drop the ball and cause more damage than the damage that has already been done.

Chapter Nine
MYRON

Myron was a young man I met about a year before my incarceration. He was a friend of Betty, who had been working with me in the small business I was running. He had a great singing voice and knew about the music school I was running. Betty told me that he was good at cleaning carpet, so I got him to clean the carpet of the studio in my apartment. Everyone who knows me knows that I'm very anal-retentive about cleanliness. That's one thing I've always wanted, to keep a clean home studio.

So Myron came one Saturday evening and started doing what he did. And we started getting into a conversation, as men do. We talked about music, and about what type of music he liked to sing. We talked about his church, and about him being part of the music ministry there. And we talked about women. We were just bonding as Christian men while he cleaned the carpet.

When he was done, he told me the price, and I wrote him a check from my business. Then we chatted a little longer as he packed up his equipment. In my mind, I was glad to meet a new friend who didn't know at the time I was going through something. I did tell him that I was separated and was trying to get my wife back, and he told me that he had been married before as well, and knew how it was. So again, we build camaraderie, and hopefully a friendship that would last.

As time went on, we would talk and chat here and there. As I said, he sang and had a great voice—a tenor voice, to be exact—and we actually had a chance to practice a song one day in my apartment. We then talked about how he'd like to sing in his church. So I suggested that we learn a song, or that I learn one of the songs that he liked, and if he wanted to sing it in his church, then I'd come one Sunday, if it was OK with his pastor, and accompany him.

The summer was coming and we continued our friendship. I was actually in between jobs, having resigned from one, and was receiving unemployment. But the funny thing was that I was on unemployment for only a short time, because a temp job became available. And you can't say no, because if they find out, they will make you pay back the money.

I took the assignment. It was at one of the Baltimore technical colleges, and I had the fun job of going through all their files and making sure everything was in order, as they were getting ready for an audit from the state. Well, during my assignment at that college was when I was called and told that there was a warrant out for my arrest. I couldn't believe it, and didn't want to believe it. I called my wife, and she called her best friend, and I called my best friend, so we could figure out what was going on.

So I gave myself up, and was in BDF. And all I was thinking about as I was doing God's will in there was when I was going to be bailed out. My wife was working on the lawyer and trying to see how she was going to get me out, and I was on the inside, trying to make calls the best way I could to anyone who would help me. Well, one call I made was to Myron. I got his number from my friend, wrote it down, and was able to call him in the evenings because he worked. I called and asked him if he would help my wife with the bail money. He said he would see what he could do. So I continued to pray and fast while I was there, and also continued to read my word.

Then one day, when it was visiting time, I got a surprise—they called my name. I couldn't even imagine who it was that came to see me. It was Myron. When I saw him, it was like a breath of fresh air. He came, we talked, and he told me some stories about himself and how he had been in trouble before, and then he prayed with me. That was the best part, him coming to visit me and praying with me. I needed that. God knew that I needed to know that someone cared enough about me to take time out of his busy schedule to come visit me. And that was not his only visit, he came back a second time as well. It's kind of funny when you think about it. A man I had recently met came to visit me, and was one of my only visitors besides my wife, and my pastor never came or even wrote.

The next thing Myron helped out with was the bail money. He got some money together and needed to hook up with my wife so that he could get it to her. I contacted her and told her to call him and meet him, so she could get the money, take it to a bail bondsman, and get me out. Well, life has a way of taking funny turns. When she got the money, and found the bail bondsman on Eastern Avenue, they wouldn't bail me out because of the charge. There I was, orchestrating everything from the inside to get out, and they wouldn't help. Unbelievable. It just goes to show you that society picks and chooses which sins are OK. I was still locked up in BDF.

My wife called Myron to tell him what happened, and she met him another time in order to return the money. But the things I appreciated about him were that he came to see me, he was willing to help, and he got the money together to help my wife in a hard situation at the time. That will always be with me. He couldn't understand either why they wouldn't bail me out. I still thanked him for trying. He was the only one to take the initiative to go even that far, so I was very grateful to him for his help and his friendship.

POEM
MISSED

I miss that person I used to be before all this craziness happened to me.

The person who grew up knowing the Lord;

The person who was constantly being instructed by His daily word…

Chapter Ten

BAIL

In BDF, they have bail reviews each morning, which I knew nothing about. The first day I was there, I listened to the others around me, and when I heard some of the horror stories, fear set in. I was in a strange land, and I couldn't even imagine what would go on if someone found out my charge. They did ask me if I wanted to go to the bail review, and I opted out. But that wasn't a good idea, because when my wife came to see me after my first week in, she told me that she and a couple of others had been there and were looking for me. They were there for support, but again, I didn't know. She said that the judge might have listened to them on my behalf, but again, I didn't know. I had fear like nothing in this world. I was in a strange land, knew no one, and then had to worry about who would find out my charge and might want to hurt me. No thank you, I'll take door number two, and work on being safe while I'm going through this trial in my life.

I continued to call her, to see how she was doing with getting the bail money together, and what she was going through. It was all getting to her: the bills, worrying about me, and just trying to hold it together so that no one would know what was going on with me. It wasn't until I'd been in for about two weeks that she broke and told somebody. You see, all who knew were trying to keep it a secret because they thought I was going to get out on bail. Heck, it was my first time being locked up, and who could have known that I wasn't coming back anytime soon?

I prayed, read my word, and continued to stay steadfast for the Lord. I kept doing the Bible studies even though I didn't want to be there. Did I mention that I didn't want to be there, just in case you didn't catch it the first time?

Now, the funny thing about being locked up is that no one should ever know what you're locked up for, unless you tell them, and at that point in my life, I wouldn't have told the fly on the wall. I wanted them to know me by my heart, not by what I did. But as time went on, and I was in there longer than expected, my cell mate came to me and said, "Everyone deserves a second chance." That made me realize that he knew what my charge was. He was nice enough to share his stuff from the commissary with me, and even brought me some for myself. He also brought me some shaving powder because I hadn't shaved for weeks, which wasn't good for me. He was a godsend. I did write to my church for help, but it was to no avail.

He even wanted to help me get bailed out. He made some calls, talked to some people, and told me to just chill. So I was patient; I waited for days and weeks, and was wondering what was going on. He then came to tell me that they didn't want to help because of the charge. So again, I couldn't get out because of the charge that I had. Heck, I was surrounded by people that had done some type of crime, but because mine was a sexual crime, I was like a leper, and no one wanted to touch me or wanted any part of me.

I did ask the church if they'd bail me out, but my wife told me that they said, "How will he pay us back?" Mind you, I'd been with that church for five to seven years, and now that I'd fallen and was in trouble, they didn't want to help me. I did write the pastor and told him that I had only one pair of underwear, and wanted them to send me a little money for the commissary so I could get at least another pair. Did that happen? No. So I continued to wash the only pair of socks and underwear I had. I also submitted slips to BDF, telling them that I had only one pair of underwear, but that, too, was to no avail.

So you see, my getting out was not on God's agenda. He needed me to be still and wait this one out. He knew there were some things happening on the outside that I needed to be safe from. He knew I wasn't ready to handle whatever my wife was doing with her ex-husband. So he kept me safe in the safest place He knew: BDF. That way, I could continue to saturate myself with His word, build up my spiritual life, and be ready for whatever I had to face when I came out. So He basically said bail was not an option for Kai. When I went in, I wasn't well equipped, but when I came out, I was more equipped for my next journey.

Chapter Eleven
THE GLASS

I watched a movie today, and it brought something to mind. It was a movie about someone who was committing check fraud and wasn't getting caught. When he finally got caught, near the end of the movie, he got a visit from the FBI agent who caught him. The scene triggered the memory of the first time my wife came to see me while I was incarcerated in the Baltimore Detention Facility.

It was a week and a half later that she finally got a chance to come see me. And when I went to the visitation room, it was all an eye-opener to me. I was on one side of the glass and she was on the other. The only way we could communicate was through the use of the phone system, and I was told by the other inmates that those things were bugged. If you said anything important, it could be used against you in court, because they were taping every conversation. So I tried not to say anything important to her because of that.

She looked at me and smiled. She noticed I had gotten my dreads cut off, which she didn't like anyway, and said I looked good. You only get a half hour to visit each time, so we talked about my best friend and her husband helping move my things out of the apartment and putting them in storage. We talked about the option of getting out on bail, or an attorney to help with the case. We chose to go with the attorney so I could have someone help with the case when I went to court. I asked her how the kids were doing, and she told me they were fine, and that she was trying to keep everything going without anyone getting suspicious. Her mom didn't know, nor did the kids know. She told me about the phone system and said she had put some money on it so that I could call her, and I thanked her for that. It was hard seeing my wife on the other side of the glass and not being able to touch her. We touched the glass, as if our hands were meeting and feeling each other. If that was all we could do for now, I was OK with that, because at least she came to see me and made sure that I was OK. We talked a little more, I prayed with her, and then it was time for her to go. She told me that she would be back the next week.

Just that little gesture of her coming to see me gave me some inner peace, and I was falling more and more in love with her because she was working on getting me out of there. You see, before we got to this unfortunate circumstance, we were falling in love for the first time in our relationship. She was glowing and I was glowing, and I loved it. I even remember when we went to get a pedicure together that same summer, and the young man that was working on her feet and mine saw the look in our eyes and said, "New love"—and that was right. We fell in love and never wanted to be apart.

She did come the next week to bring me information on the attorney that would be contacting me. She also gave me updates of what was going on in the outside world. When you're locked up in the Baltimore Detention Facility, you don't know what's going on in the real world because you're secluded from everything. The only entertainment was the television.

But something odd started happening with her visits. They started getting farther and farther apart, and I couldn't figure out why. I was under the impression that a lot was going on and she couldn't get up like she wanted.

I remember one visit that, when she finally got there, I was about to cry, because even though I was in there doing the work of the Lord, I needed to see my wife. When she saw me, she told me that she didn't want me to cry, she wanted me to be strong. She said if I cried, she would leave, so I didn't, because I needed that visit from her. She didn't know I was at that point where, if I hadn't seen her in a while and she had told me she was coming, I was always ready, sitting on one of the stairs in the facility, watching the clock, and when she didn't show it was a letdown. You start to hear names of other inmates being called for visitation, and you're the only one whose name isn't called. But I stayed in the word so that I could keep my strength up for Him.

As I think about it, the glass was the start of the real separation that was about to come. I didn't know I'd be divorcing my wife down the road because of adultery. I didn't know she was secretly having an affair with her ex-husband. That was why the visits got more and more infrequent. More of her time was being devoted to him, and I was basically getting shifted out of the picture. To me, the glass was showing that, sooner or later, you will no longer have any connection to your wife; you'll see her, but you will no longer be connected to her. And I hated that. I will always remember September 20, 2009; it was the last time we truly made love before I turned myself in. She said to me, "What if the Lord has a prison ministry for you?" Did I ever know what she meant by that? No. All I know is that the glass meant a lot of things, and that was a learning experience for me.

Chapter Twelve
JUST LIKE JUDAS

For the past few weeks I've been having so many different thoughts that I haven't had the energy to write them all down. One night while lying in my room on Edmondson Avenue a thought came to me about Judas Iscariot. When Judas betrayed Jesus and the realization of what he had done hit him, he was ashamed. The thought came to him of what he had done for thirty pieces of silver. He didn't know how to handle those emotions that came over him. It was the worst thing anyone could ever do, betray Jesus, the one he had followed and learned from for three years of Jesus's ministry. When he realized what he had done, he went back and wanted to fix it. That is the same thing we do: we sin, realize it, and then try to fix it. But they didn't want the silver back because it was Judas's guilt and problem, not theirs.

Being ashamed of what he did, Judas couldn't handle the embarrassment that went with it. The reason I know this is because I felt the same way. I was embarrassed because I had betrayed not only my family, but first and foremost, my Lord and Savior, Jesus Christ. I, too, wanted to kill myself once the realization of what I had done hit me. People were looking at me funny, my family was broken up, and the ministry of music was about to be taken away from me. I wished I was dead, just as Judas had. But I'm chicken and didn't want to end my life that way. Satan wanted me to commit suicide so that I wouldn't make it into heaven. Satan had a glimpse into my future and had seen what I could become if I overcame this hit.

You see, I believe if Judas had gone to the Jesus he knew and loved, and asked Jesus to forgive him, Jesus would have forgiven him, just like the thief on the cross. But Judas was so ashamed of what he had done that Satan got to him and tricked him into hanging himself. His life ended just the way Satan wanted it to end, in defeat and eternal damnation.

But then God, my God, had a plan for Kai. He wanted Kai to find his way back to Him. He wanted me, Kai, to find my way back to where I had been, and what I used to be, and to know that after I asked for forgiveness for what I had done, I would be welcomed back into His kingdom. Jesus was waiting for me to turn back to Him and give Him my all, and He forgave me and had a plan for my life. It was no longer my plan, but His. I've learned to take me out of it and put God first.

Chapter Thirteen
BIBLE STUDIES

The one thing that I did miss while in BDF was church and Bible study. I filled out the forms to go to Bible study during the week, but it seemed that was to no avail. I also filled out the forms to go to church, and that was to no avail also. The few months I'd been there, I had never missed church that much in my whole life. Instead, the Lord had me have Bible study in my cell. The way it happened was like this.

One day as I was waiting for my wife to visit, a new inmate came over to me and asked if I was a Christian. An odd look came over my face because I wasn't doing anything but sitting on the step, watching the clock and waiting to hear my name. So I told him yes, and then he asked me if I was having Bible studies. I looked at him and said yes. I didn't know what I was going to teach, but I knew God would give me what He wanted me to talk about.

My name was called for my visit, so I went and spent time with my wife in the visiting quarters. It was hard the first time, to see her on the other side of the glass and not be able to touch her while talking to her on the phone. She told me everything that was going on and how the kids were doing. I wanted to cry, but she told me not to. When she saw me for the first time, I had had all the dreads cut off. She said my new cut looked good. I told her that when I had a chance to get a cut, I said to cut them off. They thought I was crazy, but I said it was only hair, and I knew it would be too much to try to maintain while in there. Also, I knew that it was time. God told me he was preparing me to do His will, not my own.

I told my wife that what she said before I went in was true. She told me that when we found out that I had to go in, I might have a prison experience, and I said it had begun. The Lord was having me do Bible studies with inmates practically every night. When my visit was over, I prayed with her, told her I loved her, and then she left.

The studies began with just a small group, and then they began to grow as more inmates kept coming in. Every time a new inmate would come in, the other inmates would tell him about me, and he would come to me and ask if I was having Bible study. The first Bible study I had, I spoke on Hebrews chapter 11, the faith chapter. I read it several times, took notes, prayed, and began preaching to the sheep that the Lord gave me to teach. A few of them gave their lives to Christ. As I prayed for them, many started getting bailed out, one by one. I just couldn't understand it. I wanted to get out, but as everybody seemed to be released, I was still left in there.

Chapter Fourteen
YOUNG TIMOTHY

During my time in BDF, the Lord gave me a young man to disciple. Why, I didn't know, and to this day I still don't know. I named him Timothy. You see, he told me he was in for attempted robbery, and that broke my heart. Timothy was one of a great bunch of our black youths that get caught up in the things that the outside world makes glamorous, and then they get sent to jail when they're caught and have to do adult time. When I saw it, I didn't like it. But Timothy became special to me. He started coming to the Bible studies I held, and was always asking questions. He started reading his word daily, and at one point, I explained fasting to him and he was very receptive to it. I told him that I learned fasting from my church, and that we'd do the Daniel fast at the beginning of every new year, to start the year off right with God.

Timothy took that and ran with it. He would read, fast, and pray. We'd pray together, and he was always willing to learn more. There were even times he'd be fasting for what was going on in his life, and the things he was asking God to help him with. He would bring me his food, telling me he was fasting and asking me if I wanted it. I'd never had anyone do that for me, and I did take it and kept him in prayer. I will tell you this, I saw this six-foot-four-inch teenager grow into a fine Christian young man, right before my eyes, in less than the eighty-six days I was there. He grew so much spiritually that he was ready and willing to accept any sentence the judge gave him. I was amazed, because I never knew that the Lord would use me in such a way.

The day came that I wasn't ready for or even expecting, but it came. He had heard some things through the grapevine, as they say, about my past and what I was charged with. So he came to me and wanted to have a meeting in my cell privately. He came to me man to man, and asked me to be honest with him, and said my answer would not change the way he felt about me. I said, "OK, ask away." He wanted to know what I was in for, so I told him. He looked at me, thanked me for being honest with him, and told me that it wouldn't change our relationship. Deep down inside, I think that made our relationship stronger. You see, he needed to see a man of God be honest about his mistakes in life and not try to hide them.

When it was time for him to go to court, we would always get together and pray. There were times we'd have a prayer for everyone that was in our tier. There were also times where we'd have big circle prayers at the end of the night, before we all went to sleep. I found out that men do turn to God when they're locked up. You have time to do some soul-searching, you have time to get close to God, you have time to share your experiences. So my little Timothy was always ready to read, pray, ask questions, and meditate on the word. He was ready to accept whatever the Lord allowed to come his way. He even told his mom about me. She was worried, but he told her not to, because God was taking care of him. And just think, he was the only person I told during the whole eighty-six days I was there, and God used him to show me that there are people you can trust. But first he had to see my heart in action, and see God's light shining in me.

Thank you, Timothy, God used you to save me…

Chapter Fifteen
TWO BROTHERS

In the beginning of the year 2009, I heard from my brother. He told me that he'd been through a lot. He lost his job and fell into a deep depression. He said he had been there for over twenty-three years, and they gave him his pink slip, a good severance pay, and let him go. He said that after they let him go, he went home and stayed in bed for about a week or so, without getting out. He told me that he messed and urinated on himself, and lay in that for about a week as well. Then his best friend came in, got him cleaned up, and started helping him get his life back in order. That's a real friend, someone who won't judge you but will be there to support you.

He told me that he had used his severance pay to pay his rent for a year, and had some to chill with while he looked for a job, and that was a good idea. Meanwhile, at the end of 2009 was when the storm happened in my life. That was when my life started falling apart, after I thought that a new love had developed between my wife and me. It was then that the law had a warrant out for my arrest for sexual abuse of a minor. So, instead of them coming to find me, I got on the phone on September 17, 2009, and told them that I would turn myself in.

I was in BDF for eighty-six days, not knowing my brother was trying to find me. My numbers changed, my wife gave my phone to her daughter, and my life was slowly falling apart. It was as if I was about to be erased. Have you ever had the feeling that life was trying to erase you? I did when all this was happening to me and I had no one to help me, no one to visit me, and no one to support me. My brother and I were both going through bad times and we didn't even know it. Brothers and sisters should never go through storms in their lives with neither of them knowing about it. But the problem was that my brother and I were never close. He left Philadelphia when I was a little thirteen-year-old kid just trying to make it through life. He left and moved to Baltimore. He never said good-bye, didn't call much, and didn't write much. He was just gone. It was as if he abandoned me and went about his life in his world. My mother always had communication with him, but I didn't. The funny thing is that we grew up close, we had fun. My older cousin Tiffany was always around as well. They, along with my mother and grandmother, were my family. But somewhere down the road Satan didn't like what was going on in my life. I think he peeked into my future and decided he was going to upset my fruit basket and leave Kai to make it in the world all by himself. You see, family is important. If your family is dispersed, you're left alone, living life alone, trying every day to survive. That was me. At the age of ten my life was turned upside down, and I was left to grow up to become either the man that Satan wanted me to be or the man of God that God wanted me to be. That was my life's struggle for the past twenty-three years.

You see, abandonment has always been an issue with me. No one in my life has ever had staying power. People have come and people have gone, family included. Like I said, I had a family of my own till the age of ten, and then life's struggles hit the family and I had to go and live with was my aunt and her family. I went from living with just a few people in a household to living in large family conditions where I had to basically share everything because life was much different.

What I'm basically saying is that my brother and I hadn't really talked to each other like brothers for over thirty-five years or so. Life has this funny way of sneaking up on you and disappointing you. He left, I had no brother, my mother and father were alcoholics, and I was left to try to live my life and make it. I had no guidance from a brother or a father. My father was married to my stepmother, and my brother and sister on my father's side had him. I had a father, but they had a daddy. I never knew what a daddy was because he had more children than he could afford. He and my brother never saw eye to eye, and somewhere deep down inside I knew my brother had a hatred for my father because of how he used to abuse my mother. Yes, I've actually seen him beat her and slap her around and drag her by her hair when they were drunk and fighting. That is one of the main reasons why I've never been drunk because I saw what it did to the people I loved. For the first time in my life, as I write this I'm crying about it, because being a grown man now I understand what was going on. Alcohol was one of the things that destroyed my family and took my mother as well as my father away from me.

But getting back to the two brothers: you see, after I got out of BDF, I did start looking for my brother, but I couldn't find him. I looked on the Internet, but it was to no avail. I looked on Facebook, but he's not very computer literate, so that was a no go. I tried to search for family members that may have known where he was, but I lost contact with my Baltimore family as well. I got lost in my mess and couldn't find anyone. After my last marriage went belly up, I was alone again, wanting to find my brother and praying to God that he wasn't dead. After everything I'd been through, that was one thing I knew I wouldn't be able to handle. I lost my mother and my father (who I'd basically never had a relationship with); to lose my brother would have been devastating. Once again, God proved that he was in my life and did a miracle. After three years of sickness, imprisonment, probation, and a divorce, my brother found me. The day after my mother's seventy-second birthday, on July 19, 2012, I received an e-mail from my brother's best friend, telling me that he had been looking for me, and he didn't know that I was looking for him. The ironic thing is that I was just Googling him again that morning at work, but God being God did His thing and made it all come together. I thank God for that miracle, because it was only Him that, in the right time, brought us back together as brothers. He knows that my brother needs me and I need him. We may not be on the same page right now, we may not go to church together, we may not worship together, but he's my brother and I love him dearly, and I won't let him go.

Chapter Sixteen

EIGHTY-SIX DAYS OF INTIMACY

When I was locked up for eighty-six days in BDF, I had nothing to do but read and study the word of God. I did more reading and studying of His word than I did my entire existence on this earth. I was really getting to know God and who He really was in my life. You see, we men want to get intimate with that special young lady, and you women want to get intimate with that special young man. But in many cases, you don't get to really know that man or that woman. We're looking for intimacy, but we're not looking to be friends with that person. We're looking for love. As we're looking for that love, nine times out of ten it becomes lust first, and the friendship and love factor goes out the door.

The experience I had for eighty-six days: I had no radio, no hustle and bustle of daily routines, didn't have to go to work, didn't have to wash dishes, and didn't have to daily life things.

The first thing on my mind was getting out of there ASAP, but Daddy wasn't having it. There was a lesson that had to be learned, there was some breaking that had to be done, and He didn't need any distractions that life brings to hinder that. He needed me to be alone with Him and others that needed to know Him. He needed me to be the salt and light in a dark place of men that were lost. I didn't want to be there, but I had no choice. For the first time in my life I wasn't in control of what was happening to me. It was a feeling of dread. It was a feeling of being lost and surrounded by many spirits, and in danger of being hurt. But I did what He wanted me to do. I found a Bible that belonged to someone else who got in trouble for fighting, and started my grind. I read, and read, and read. Man, I read the story of David and Goliath, the story of Gideon, and many of the New Testament scriptures. I read about Paul and started feeling that I had something in common with him. As I meditate upon it now, it was the beginning of a real intimate relationship with my Heavenly Father.

I prayed in the morning, I prayed before I went to sleep, I prayed at dinner. When times were getting rough, I started singing hymns in my cell. I sang what praise songs I remembered and continued to stay in the spirit. For the first time in all my forty-six years of living, I was having a real relationship with my Creator. He took this time in my life to humble me and to use me to be the salt and light to those around me.

The funny thing is that during my stay there, I put in cards to request to go to Bible study, but that never happened. I put in a request to go to church, but it was to no avail. So I was obedient to God, and when people would ask if I was having a Bible study in the evening, I said yes, and asked Him to please give me what He wanted me to feed those lost souls. So the Bible studies began, and when they did, it required me to read, pray, and study even more so that I could be ready to feed the sheep that were around me. Trust me, I didn't want to do that. I wanted out! Every time a new inmate would come in, he would somehow find his way to me and ask if I was doing a Bible study. I'd say yes and tell him what cell I was in. God used that time for me to get closer to Him, and also gave me a yearning for others. I began to look at people's hearts rather than the outside stuff they got caught up in. Why? Because I myself found out how easy it is to get caught up in sin and not be aware of its outcome. It is so true what the word says, "For the wages of sin is death" (Romans 6:23), and God had to humble me so that I would be able to follow the calling He had on my life. Oh, yeah, I also taught others that wanted to really get to know Christ how to fast. Fasting was part of my life before I went in and I didn't want it to stop.

I could not believe the times when inmates would wake me up early in the morning and ask me to pray for them before they went to court. I never knew that would happen. I remember Jonathan, a white male who was in for conspiracy and the law was trying hard to get him. He knew a lot about law, and was reading law books and helping others along the way, but to make a long story short, he even came to me before he went to court and asked me to pray for him. So what do you do? You pray. In eighty-six days I'd gotten closer to my Lord and Savior, and He used me and allowed me to be tested, because you know God does not test, but He will allow it (James 1:12–15). The harder I tried to get out on bail, the more He used me inside there. At the time, I even told my wife that I had one more test, and I knew I would not be released until I passed this last and final test.

Mr. Gray was that test. This young man came in and saw that I was a God-fearing man, and he started emulating me. But I found out from careful study that he'd been incarcerated before, and it showed. He had that jail mentality. But anyway, he saw my little desk that I made up with my open Bible on it. He liked that and made one for himself. Now mind you, Mr. Gray would proclaim that he was a Christian and a God-fearing man, but he would slip up with a cuss word here or there. So I brought back in that old slogan: 99.5 percent won't do, you have to be 100 percent for God.

He would stop and say, "You're right," and then we'd pray. I remember the times when it was mealtime and I'd get the plate with the most food on it, and he would always say, "Yeah, you want the most food." I would tell him, "Here, if this is what you want, then take it." You see, God had taught me to be humble in my humbling circumstances. I was not going to argue over who had the biggest piece of chicken. I wanted him to understand that I was not that type of person, and was at a different level in my life, and I always wanted to show love.

I also remember the times he'd call his girlfriend, who he wanted to marry, and ask me to speak to her. So I did, giving her some good news on him. Or he would ask her to do me a favor and contact my wife when it was difficult for me to reach her; that was greatly appreciated. But I did what I always did, tried to continue to show him love, even when it was difficult and he was getting on my last nerves at times. But I think underneath he was a kind person; he was just caught up in the things of the world and didn't want to let them go. Trust me, I always kept an eye on him. As the word says, we must try spirits by the spirit (1 John 4:1). I needed to know what spirit was at work at any given moment.

I remember a time when he went to court and I didn't think he was coming back, so we got his cell. Well, before we knew it he came back, and he was highly upset because of the cell change. I think his day in court didn't go as well as he planned, and I saw another side of him that I didn't expect to see. But let me back up a minute. I found out one thing while I was incarcerated, and that is: information that is supposed to be kept personal or secret from the other inmates always seems to be leaked. You see, since I was in for a sexual crime against a minor, they asked if I wanted to go into protective custody. Thinking that I was only going to be in there for a couple of weeks at the most, I said no and was put in regular population. Again, I thought it was going to be a short stay, but who knows? Sometimes we think things aren't really the way they are.

So Mr. Gray was always trying to figure me out, or figure out what I was in there for, because I didn't fit the profile of those that were in there. It was probably driving him crazy. So he went and found out, and after a minute he started giving subtle hints to others, but they wouldn't believe him. But he did talk to my little Timothy, the young man I took under my wing. I was teaching him God's word, praying with him, and teaching him about fasting and why we fast. He was yearning for the word and I was there for him, which was God's design, not mine.

But anyway, back to Mr. Gray. When Mr. Gray found out what had happened, his old spirit arose in him and he wanted to fight me. Since I knew what happened if you fought, I didn't even worry about it, but my young Timothy was ready to fight for me. So I had to take him aside and tell him that sometimes it's better to take the low road than to travel the high road. I didn't want him to get into trouble because of me, and I wasn't going to let him. He calmed down and we prayed, and he was cool after that. I must admit that it was the first time anyone was ready to fight on my behalf. Now I know what Jesus felt like when Peter cut off the guard's ear. We are to live in peace and not war. This is one part of the story I will never forget: that a young man was ready to fight for me so that I wouldn't get hurt.

Chapter Seventeen
THE COVENANT

As I was studying my word during my stay at BDF, I read many scriptures where God was talking to his people and made covenants with many of them. He made a covenant with Abraham and told him that he was going to be a father of many nations. The two spies made a covenant with the prostitute Rehab for helping them, and her family was saved when the city of Jericho was destroyed. So what did I do? I looked up the meaning of covenant, and here is what it said. A covenant is an agreement, usually formal, between two or more persons to do or not do something specified. So when God makes a covenant of agreement with anyone, He always sticks to what he says. He's not one to go against His word.

I kept reading and studying, and saw more and more when God was making covenants with His people because of His love for them. So one night I got down on my knees and talked to Him like I'd never talked to Him before. I needed to know and understand what He wanted from me, and what He wanted me to do for the rest of my life for Him. At that moment, I was tired of always telling God that I was going to stop doing this and stop doing that. We all do that, and what do we do? We end up doing it anyway. Well, when you make a promise to someone, especially Him, you should always try your best to stick to it because again, when He makes a promise, He never goes against His word.

I told God that when He felt it was time for me to be released, I would do two things. One, I would preach His word, because I knew he'd given me a calling to preach His word to others. I knew he'd kept me in there to learn how to love others when I really didn't want to because of my circumstances. We all must admit that when we're going through tough times, we don't want to love anyone else. We're just worried about getting through our problem, weathering the storm, winning this war we're in. But I knew in my heart that I had to stop running from Him, and do what He'd called me to do: to preach the word, in season and out. And you know what? It was not going to be hard because that was what I'd done the whole time I was in there. I was witnessing, I was praying, I was fasting, and I preached. Many times I didn't want to, but I did these things to please Him.

Secondly, I told him that when I was released I would take care of my family. I made that covenant because I knew I didn't do it right the first time, and I was ready to do it right. But I didn't know that while I was inside for eighty-six days my family was slowly being taken away from me. That was a hard pill to swallow. But then I had to think. I said I would take care of my family, but I didn't specifically say what family.

So, with all that's happened in the past few years, the divorce and losing that family I think God is preparing me for something new in my life, even with all the circumstances that are going on now. He never goes back on His word, and I'm going to continue to stand on His promise.

I've grown tremendously since that experience, and I wouldn't change it for all the tea in China because it opened my eyes, my heart, and my spirit to God's way of thinking. I'm walking in His light now and won't turn back. He's brought me back to Kai, the one I lost many years ago. He's kept me celibate for several years now because my life belongs to Him; it's not mine anymore. I'm living, breathing, and testifying for Him. Several years ago, I heard a preacher say that we're living epistles. When people see us, they should see the Christ in us, and that's where my life is now. Those two covenants that I made with Christ will always be in the forefront of my life. And the funny thing is that today the pastor preached a great sermon and reminded us that the promises, the covenants, and the agreements we made with God, and He with us, will never be unrewarded. That's all I needed to hear. That was my confirmation of my covenants with Him, and with the help of the Holy Spirit, I'm going to keep them.

POEM

SO DON'T THROW AWAY YOUR BOLD FAITH

Hebrews 10:35

- ☑ So don't throw away your bold faith. It will bring you rich rewards…**A renewed marriage.**

- ☑ So don't throw away your bold faith. It will bring you rich rewards…**A new love for your spouse.**

- ☑ So don't throw away your bold faith. It will bring you rich rewards…**Peace in the midst of your storm.**

- ☑ So don't throw away your bold faith. It will bring you rich rewards…**Hearing your wife say she's proud of you as you go through the storm.**

- ☑ So don't throw away your bold faith. It will bring you rich rewards…**As you preach the word people's faith is strengthened.**

- ☑ So don't throw away your bold faith. It will bring you rich rewards…**As you preach the word people's shackles are being let loose one by one.**

- ☑ So don't throw away your bold faith. It will bring you rich rewards…**You are being saturated with God's word daily.**

- ☑ So don't throw away your bold faith. It will bring you rich rewards…**The church calling out "Hezekiah" in a corporate prayer at the Thanksgiving Eve service.**

- ☑ So don't throw away your bold faith. It will bring you rich rewards…**The patience to deal with others and their shortcomings.**

- ☑ So don't throw away your bold faith. It will bring you rich rewards…**The hope of knowing your release is soon.**

- ☑ So don't throw away your bold faith. It will bring you rich rewards…**When you go from tribulation to triumph.**

- ☑ **So don't throw away your BOLD FAITH!**

Written: December 3, 2009

Chapter Eighteen
THE REGISTRATION

On December 17, 2009, as I left the courtroom after receiving my adjusted sentence of probation for three years instead of spending ten years behind bars, I was told that I was to be put on the sexual offender's registry list. I was told by my lawyer that I would only be on there a short period of time, and then I'd be taken off. This was actually a plea bargain. My wife told me that my stepdaughter didn't want to testify, but being that I was inside and couldn't do anything to help myself, I was at the hands of the DA, who didn't know the whole story because no one wanted to hear my side of what had happened, or even how I sought help for myself. All they wanted was another notch in their belt. They wanted me on the list, to destroy my life and humiliate me.

They gave me my papers and released me, and after getting a couple of bus tokens to get back to civilization, I went on my way. I was first to go to the probation office and sign up, and then I had a few days to register or they'd put me back in jail.

So I went to my best friend Tina's house and waited for her to get home. She was surprised to see me. We hugged, and I told her what had happened in the courtroom, and that my attorney said that my wife didn't want to see me. Well, while we were catching up, her phone rang and it was my wife. She said she was trying to get to me and that she didn't know where the attorney got that information from. He even told the judge that my estranged wife didn't want anything to do with me and that my stepdaughter just wanted me out and not in jail. So I talked to her and she said she'd come by soon to see me.

I had to do the main part of my sentence; I had to register with the nearest police department. I went to one of Baltimore County's police department offices and registered. When I went, they took my picture and fingerprinted me again, and then made me sign this paper of what I had to do since I was now on the registry. I read it and burst into tears. One of the conditions was that I was not able to go onto any real property of any public school. The one thing I'd done my entire life was taken away from me. I cried like there was no tomorrow. God had to really help me with that; the thing I loved was taken away from me. I loved working with children, helping them learn, and now this. The only thing I knew to do was cry. I went back to my best friend's house and meditated because I was distraught. So I've had to make a conscious effort not to go to any schools. It was hard. We're talking about a man who's been in the schools ever since he was a boy, and now, after a mistake in my life, they take that away from me. That's why it hurt.

The next things I had to deal with were the home visits, and the weekly visits to the probation office to make sure I did everything I was supposed to do to make it to the end of this three-year probation. Then, in October 2010, a new law was passed that all registrants had to be on the registry for the rest of their lives. I didn't sign up for that; it was supposed to be for ten years. But our government said that if one is bad or makes a mistake, all are bad and need to be punished. So I was saying to myself, *I'm divorced, my wife is with another man, and I'm left holding the bag for everyone's mistakes in life.* Ironic, how life works. I had to really stay in my word, pray and fast, and keep Jesus as the center of my joy, because my whole life and way of living had now taken a complete turn for the worse. Or so I thought.

So now, out of jail, on the registry, what next? I was told by my Lord and Savior to trust Him—not my wife, not the system, not the preacher—to trust Him. So I decided after all that to follow what the Lord told Joshua, son of Nun: "Don't look to the left or the right, continue to meditate on the law my servant Moses gave you and I will direct your path and you will be blessed" (Joshua 1:7–9).

Chapter Nineteen
TRANSITIONAL HELP

I chose to write this chapter because Joan, one of my best friends, told me to dig deep about the pain I went through. As I was being released, I remember saying to myself, *Where am I going?* I was told by the attorney that my wife didn't want any part of me, so I couldn't go find her. The only thought was to go to my best friend Tina's house. So after doing what was required of me, I went back to the detention center, got my belongings and a couple of free bus tokens, and headed to my best friend's house.

I made my way up the hill to the bus stop and started my journey back to where the journey began. It was strange; while detained for eighty-six days, I didn't see any light from the outside, or breathe any air from the outside. It was just inside light and air for eighty-six days. No one knew how I felt to be locked up in a place I didn't want to be and couldn't get out of, even to get some fresh air and not just detention facility air. I caught the bus.

When I got to Tina's, she wasn't home, but her kids were, so I sat, waited, and watched TV. Then, when she came home, she was surprised and gave me a hug. I told her what was said about my wife and we talked for a little bit. They ordered out and I had my first dinner with her and her family.

While I was sitting on the couch talking to her, her cell phone rang. It was my wife, and she wanted to speak to me. I was kind of skeptical about talking to her because I didn't know what to expect. She said that everything the lawyer had said was a lie; she hadn't said those things, and everything was OK between us. She said she would stop by and see me when she got a chance, so I said OK and hung up.

My best friend made up a bed for me in her son's room because he wasn't home for the holidays yet, and I had my first night's rest in a real bed on December 17, 2009.

After I got up the next morning, I had a bath, the first one in a long time, and had real food for breakfast. I had a chance to relax after my adventure of being locked up—detained. I told them some of my story about what I went through while I was incarcerated. Told them about the calling on my life to preach the word, and how I read more word in eighty-six days than I had read in my entire life. I was truly saturated with the word of God and loved it. I told them that I couldn't wait to get to church again and worship like I did before.

Well, that Sunday it came time for us to get ready for church, and lo and behold a snowstorm hit. I said, "Wow, my first time back in a while and it snows. Who would have thought that would happen in a million years?" I didn't have any money because all my accounts got messed up as a result of my being locked up, so I went out to make some money by shoveling people's sidewalks and driveways. My best friend was already letting me stay with her for free and feeding me, so I at least had to make something to help out. I went around in the cold, knocked on doors, and made some money to help out and get some of the little things I might need.

She pulled me aside one day while I was there and told me that she had a house on Baltimore Street that she was working on, and asked if I wanted to stay there as I was going through my transition. I said yes. She then discussed it with her husband, Benjamin, and we all sat down and talked about it. You see, they don't mind helping people, but only for a minute. They also don't want you to get in the habit of wanting to stay with them. They try to help you get on your feet and on your own.

So after Tina talked to Benjamin, they said I could stay there while he was working on it, but I'd have to pay the electric bill. So after I started getting unemployment that's what I did; I helped with the electric bill. But the only drawback was that there wasn't a furnace in the house yet. They only had a kerosene heater. Benjamin showed me one night how to turn it on, and then it was on and popping. They helped with a little food so that I had a start, and even got me a blow-up bed. That's true friendship, and it gave me a little push. They also helped me by giving me some dishes, pots, and pans, so I wouldn't feel like a burden on anyone. That's one thing I appreciated about Tina;

she was there to help, but not enable. She's always been a teacher to me and I've always respected her for that.

Now I had a place to stay as I was transitioning back into society after losing my home. It wasn't quite the best place to be, but it was a home for me and a blessing from God. Benjamin brought me some kerosene. I thanked him and her, and they left. I was in a new place, at a new time in my life.

I remember it clearly, as though it was yesterday. Even though I had the kerosene heater, when the kerosene ran out, it did get cold in whatever room I was in. My money was tight when I had it, so I was always trying to make the kerosene last as long as possible. I remember that it ran out one night while I was asleep, and I woke up in the middle of the night cold. I got out my bed, got the coat that I borrowed from her son, and wrapped it around me as close as possible to keep warm. It was hard for me. There I was, a man with a college degree who had lost everything, living in a home that wasn't even done. It was just a roof over my head, and cold. I cried many a time while in that home because I'd come to the conclusion that it wasn't easy, but it was a home for the time being. I was able to get food stamps and go shopping to put food in my new home, and was able to start cooking. The one thing that Benjamin wanted me to do was to help take the paint off some of the walls in my spare time, to help him get the home on the market to sell. So I did that once in a while, since they were helping me and not charging me rent.

He also helped me with getting some work until I found a real job. You see, not many people will take you in, help you get some work, and give you a roof over your head, but they did. Benjamin was contracted to remodel a home and get it ready for renting, and he asked if I wanted to help with it. I said yes and we started. He'd pay me when he got his money from the job. He said the job should last about a month. I greatly appreciated it. I had never minded working; it was just tough finding a job when I have a felony on my record. But God used these two angels who believed in me, and that was all I needed, someone who believed in me, a man who made a mistake and wasn't the monster that society was making him out to be. I will always thank God for them, and one day will pay back everything that I owe them, if not more.

Chapter Twenty

THE HILL

After being released from BDF, I could hardly wait to get to New Covenant. For the first time in my life, I hadn't been to church in over three months. I got ready at Tina's house, and her husband Benjamin drove me to church with them. When we got there, some of the congregation that had missed me came and told me I was truly missed. But I still felt like some of them didn't expect to see me there. Sunday school was going on, and I sat in the back and listened. After Sunday school, I was asked to go to the back in the trustee's room. In there, I was in front of Minister Tina, her sister, Minister Carey, Elder Mullins, and the church administrator, Charmaine.

They wanted to know the conditions of my release from BDF. I told them what I had been advised by my wife and the state's attorney, which was that I could go to church, even though we all went to the same church, as long as I didn't sit next to her daughter. When I first came in they weren't expecting me, because Elder Mullins was a captain in BDF and he was keeping them abreast of everything that was going on, or so he thought. But my wife and stepdaughter were actually more aware of what was going on than they were. Sister Charmaine asked what the judge had said and which judge I had. I told her, and she said, "You just got out, and you don't want to get in trouble, because someone may find out something and see you near the victim and call the authorities, and that won't be good." They said they loved me, but I couldn't stay in that church. My best friend Tina was devastated; she didn't know what to say or do. They told me that since I'd visited the church up the hill before, I should go there for its service.

Wow, for the first time in my life I was being put out of church. I'd been waiting three months to get back into church, and there I was, being kicked out. So I picked up my dignity and walked out, and headed up the hill to Jesus Saves Baptist Church. I walked in the door and the first person that greeted me with a smile was Elder Phineas. She remembered that I had visited before, and that I had dreadlocks, and asked me to come in and join the service, which was about to begin. She also remembered that I was a musician. And ever since that day I've been at Jesus Saves Baptist Church.

Tina called me that evening and was as upset as I was. My wife called me and said that she and the kids were upset because they were expecting to see me in the service. Tina was trying to think of ways around this whole thing, but there weren't any. Whatever was in place was to protect my stepdaughter, and to protect me so that I could get through my probation. I told Tina that I would be OK, and would just have to take it one day at a time. We prayed, and my first day back in a church was done.

Chapter Twenty-One
THE THERAPY

I decided around the month of February 2009 to go see Dr. Stephenson Cash. I've seen Dr. Cash about everything I was going through prior to the incarceration, and even told my wife to get in touch with him because he wanted to help, but she went only one time.

So I got my PAC and Dr. Cash was able to see me with no problems. We started talking about the marriage and how things were going. Dr. Cash gave me some helpful advice about making a marriage work, because we both thought that was what my wife wanted to do, make our marriage work. We talked about how I fell into the trap with my stepdaughter, and about the way little girls are made up. He explained to me that little girls at even the age of two years old may not listen to Mommy, but when Daddy walks in the room they will be very attentive to him—or even any male. So when my stepdaughter saw that I was paying attention to her, she thought that was a way of getting all the attention, even if I was her mother's husband. I didn't know what was going on. I'd been working with children my whole life, but maybe because I'd never paid attention to little girls like that had caused me to be left wide open. I'd never been in close proximity to a little girl that wasn't family. When I was with my family, I had love for the little girls like they were mine, but then I'd give them back to their parents.

Well, this little girl had made it tough for me to even get close to her, and I didn't realize that it was a trap. Dr. Cash told me all about little girls and what you have to look for. He paid close attention to me, to make sure this wasn't a behavior that might come back, or was something I enjoyed. He kept probing me and asking questions to keep me focused. He even gave me some examples of how his wife handled their granddaughter who tried to be in control. Slowly but surely, I started understanding what had happened. I asked him, as I asked another therapist, "Why did she pick me?" He said the same thing, "Because you were available." But there was still something wrong. Why would she want to pick her mother's husband? After it was discovered, and we were trying to make our family work, I tried to find a therapist that would help my stepdaughter. I'd taken her to three of them in total, all over the Baltimore area, but she wouldn't talk. I was trying to get my wife help, but she wouldn't take it either. I took us all to Dr. Cash, but I was the only one who wanted to get help.

After I was released from BDF, I worked on getting a job or some type of income to take care of myself. I called unemployment and was allotted some funds, until I had a hearing because Kennedy Services protested my getting unemployment. I then went to social services and applied for food stamps, and was accepted for two hundred dollars a month at first. I told my wife that I was approved, and that I would share some with her and the children, since she was living with her mother and needed help with groceries.

While I was in the social services office, I asked about health insurance and was told about the Primary Adult Care (PAC) program that helps those from the ages of eighteen to sixty-five with health insurance. So I applied and was accepted as well. I do thank God for allowing me all these benefits, because I know my health is important even in these times.

I decided that I had to work on me and get on the right path of life again. So I went to get help once again for the incident that had happened, and for the forthcoming divorce. I needed to talk, and to understand, and I also needed healing and to forgive myself. I needed to move on, and let God deal with me for the rest of my life, and learn how not to fall into those traps again.

Chapter Twenty-Two

THOUGHTS

Here are the thoughts I have right now in my life. I am numb. I have no desire for love because I'm at a point in my life where I've lost everything that I loved. I lost the love of the woman I learned to love unconditionally, I lost things that I've had my whole life, and I lost trust in the ones I thought I could trust. I wound up in a place that was lonely and dark; a place in my life full of evil and demonic spirits. I lost someone that I loved dearly. I lost me. I lost a friend that had a passion for life and everyone around him. I lost me. I have spurts right now of thoughts like this that I try to complete, but I'm not quite there yet. In time, I know every thought will be completed with the help of the Holy Ghost.

Chapter Twenty-Three
THE GOOD SAMARITAN

For the past few months, the story of the Good Samaritan has been in my mind, and I couldn't figure out why. Well, it just came to me: it is symbolic of what I went through. We have Good Samaritans around us every day; we just don't open our eyes to see them. When what was going on between my stepdaughter and me was discovered, it was like I was the one who got hurt. I fell into sin and needed help, but there was no help around. I was robbed of my dignity, my self-esteem, my self-worth. I was looked down on, frowned upon, and smirked at. I felt as if I was nothing.

People don't know, or even try, to care about you when you've fallen into sin, especially in the church. The church is supposed to be a place of healing, but that was not the case when I fell. Instead, the leader of the church took more interest in one of his leaders, who was an evangelist and my stepdaughter's grandmother. He was more concerned with what she wanted than with remembering his role as a pastor who takes care of all the sheep. He looked at me when I was down, and walked around.

After it was discovered, he took more time trying to bring me before the board of the church and have me tell them what I did than trying to promote healing for me or get me help to see what had brought me to that point. He was more concerned for the reputation of the church, which is a building, than for a soul that was hurting. He left the soul there on the side of the road, rather than try to help it.

When I was going through my troubles, I'd be in my apartment by myself, going to work every day, and attending another church, but the pastor never called, never came by to check on me, never even tried to send his elder to come check on me. Again, I was left by the side of the road. How is it that when someone is going through difficulties, it's so easy just to leave that person alone, with no spiritual guidance in his or her life? You're supposed to be their pastor, but you drop the ball because of fear and leave them stranded by the side of the road all alone.

How is it that, when I wrote a letter from prison, and asked for some money or even a visit, the pastor was more concerned about his reputation? How is it that he would leave me, without even a letter that his administrator could have typed up for him? How is it that, when I asked them to bail me out of jail so that I could get myself a good lawyer and get ready for court, the only thing that came to their minds was how I was going to pay them back? It was just too easy to leave me there in jail with only one pair of underwear and no money. Oh, yeah, it wasn't something that he did; that's why it was easy. But my Bible tells me that, "All have sinned and come short of the glory of God" (Romans 3:23). So I was truly left on the side of the road.

I could have hope, which I thought I did during the time I was incarcerated. I thought I had a wife that was there for me and was going to be by my side. But that, too, was a lie. She abandoned me while I was incarcerated and fell in love with her ex-husband, who was also married. I got out and there was no more love for me; it was all for him. She was doing things I'd never seen her do before. She was lying; she was staying up all night to hang out with her children's father. We would have sex, but she didn't want to get too close to me. She didn't want to kiss me, or let me hold her like I used to before I was incarcerated in September 2009. She was a totally different person. I thought I knew her, but it turned out that I didn't.

I didn't know that while I was inside BDF, she was having an affair. She was lying to me about a number of things that to this day I still don't know the whole truth about. So again, I was left by the side of the road. During my incarceration, the charade was put on so that I wouldn't suspect anything. I had fallen in love with my wife, thinking that we were going to make it through this, not knowing that God had allowed Satan to counterattack and knock out all the hope I had so that I wouldn't make it to where God wanted me to be in my life. Satan used the ones I loved to hurt me, to put me on the back burner, to put me out on the side of the road.

There should never be a time between a husband and a wife where the husband has to almost pay to have sex with his wife. That's not the way God designed it, even in sin. When a person has truly apologized and has asked God for forgiveness, if God forgives that person, it's done. Unfortunately, deep down in her heart, after she hooked up with her children's father, she changed. I knew she had changed; she had spirits in her that I'd never encountered before. For her, there was no turning back. She told me she was in love with her children's father, who by the way took her for sixteen thousand dollars in child support because of the love she confessed for him. Go figure. But again, I was abandoned and left by the side of the road.

She said she made sure I got out of jail, but she didn't realize that it was God that used her to get me out. She was always one that thought she was in control of everything, and that everyone was supposed to be scared of or fear her. But contrary to her belief, God was the one in control. He had me the whole time. Yes, I was by the side of the road, beaten up by my errors and wrong choices in life, robbed of everything, but God was still in control. So, my church passed me by, my wife passed me by, and for the first time in my life I was truly down, and didn't know what was going to happen next or who was going to help me.

When I finally got to church, I was asked to go to the trustee's room in the back before the service began. When I got to the room, I saw my best friend and her sisters, who were ministers in the church, the church administrator, and an elder. They asked me about my papers and what was said about me being near my stepdaughter. I told them that I could be in the same building with her, but couldn't be next to her. That was what my wife had told me. The elder was also a captain in the facility where I had been, and said he couldn't consciously allow that or he'd get in trouble. They were basically telling me that I had to go so I wouldn't mess up my probation. So I left in the cold, with no coat.

I was essentially kicked out of the church that Sunday, after not being in a church for over three months. I had to walk up that hill in Pikesville and go to the next church. It was humiliating, it was degrading, and it was sickening. I walked, I cried, and I sniffled till I got to the door of the other church. I got my dignity together and opened the door, and a welcoming smile greeted me at the door. She smiled and invited me in. She actually remembered that I had been there before. She gave me a program as I came in. Being the new person and not knowing anyone, I stayed in the back pew. Once again, I was a stranger in a strange land. I was alone, without my wife and children. I listened to the sermon; it was a good word. It was something I needed to hear after being locked up for three months. After the sermon I went up for prayer. Pastor Jackson prayed for me and saw something special going on in my life. I was crying up a storm and it felt good. They "knelt down and picked me up," took me to the altar for healing, and left me in the hands of my Lord and Savior.

So that was it. I started going to that church every Sunday, from that first day when I had to walk up the hill in the cold wearing beat-up leather shoes, a brown suit, and no belt. One of the elders started giving me a ride home and witnessing to me, and the men prayed for me. I began going to Tuesday night Bible studies, and moving closer and closer to the front of the church. There was love there; they loved me, and didn't know or even care about my past. They showed true, godly, Jesus Christ kind of love; the real love that I needed in my life, not fake love. It was 100 percent love from the Father up above. That church was and is the Good Samaritan that God used to bring healing to my life and soul. I will ever be grateful to my Heavenly Father for allowing them to help me, heal me, and know true church love. Eventually, Jesus Saves Baptist Church became my new church family and one that I will cherish forever.

Chapter Twenty-Four

THREE YEARS AND EIGHTY-SIX DAYS

The title of this chapter means a lot: it's the time that the pastor had before I was incarcerated to truly be a pastor to me. This is the time he had to take me in and get to know me, and help me figure out what had happened. This was the time he had to pray with me, teach me, and lead me, as a pastor should do. You see, after the discovery I was basically left out in the wilderness for three years before my incarceration and for the eighty-six days I was incarcerated. I've always thought that when a person falls into sin, it's the pastor's job to help bring that person back and put a hedge around him or her. I felt that I was left all alone, and that he didn't want to have anything to do with me because of the type of sin I committed.

The elder of the church did the same thing as well. I was looking for support from the men in the church and there wasn't any. Why would you leave a man all alone, with no support from any brothers? When a brother or sister of the faith is in need of help, we need to surround and pray for him or her. That was a critical time in my life where I needed guidance, so that I wouldn't do anything else I didn't need to do. But it didn't happen. Yes, I was wrong, and I admit it. But as Christians we need to help each other when we fall into sin. No one is perfect yet (Matthew 5:48), and we need to always keep that in the back of our minds. I'd played the piano for the church for over five years, and was always there when they needed me, but in my time of need, I was left out in my wilderness by myself. I'm not understanding that; is it a requirement of a pastor, that when something you don't understand happens, you just up and run, or don't try to get help for the person? It could be a soul that may be lost in the depths of hell, and you let it go.

I now know how the Israelites felt when they had to walk in the wilderness for over forty years. You're lost, you're seeking, you're wondering, and people are gossiping, staring, and not even caring about you. No one's calling to see if you're OK, if you need anything. You're just all on your own, left for God to have His way with you, where you either let Him or continue to do it on your own.

The police discovered what happened three years later and then I was incarcerated. I didn't want to go, but when a warrant was put out for my arrest, I turned myself in, hoping they would be lenient with me. Well, as we know, the system is not like that. They thought I was a runner and decided to put a seventy-five-thousand-dollar bond on me. My wife and best friend tried to hide it from everyone, but it got to the point where they couldn't get me out on bail and it had to be revealed. And even at that moment, when the pastor found out, he had a chance to help, but he didn't. It's as if he didn't want anything to do with me. He didn't want his name in anything. I wrote him a letter asking for his help to bail me out, and to send me some money because I had only one pair of underwear, but it was to no avail. I even asked for a visit, and he never came. He was scared that he might be seen coming to see me. Wow, I was one of his sheep, and he didn't want to come see me. My wife said they didn't want to bail me out because they didn't know how I would pay them back.

I was incarcerated for eighty-six days with only one pair of underwear, which I had to learn to wash pretty often if I wanted it fresh once in a while. Had no money because the wife was on the outside acting up with her ex-husband without my knowledge, and couldn't even afford to bring me twenty dollars to get a pair of underwear from the commissary. I would have had nothing, if it wasn't for the Lord putting on the heart of a cell mate to help me out with the commissary. Even after he found out what my crime was, he said that everyone deserved a second chance. He even got me some shaving products because my hair was growing on my face and messing it all up. Even though I was left without help from the outside, God made it possible that I would receive help from the inside. No one wanted to help the man who had sinned and didn't have any money to help himself. The funny thing is that a pastor from Africa came to see one of his congregants who had been locked up for selling drugs. He came all the way from Africa once he heard; my pastor only had to drive maybe twenty minutes down the road and wouldn't do it.

So he had three years and eighty-six days to show love, or come see me, or even pray with me, hug me, or tell me it was going to be OK, but he chose to do none of the above. What I'm hoping is that we all read and meditate on what I've written so that we don't leave anyone out, because we don't know what people may do if they're left alone and not loved. Please show love even to the least of these (Matthew 25:40), because they will need it. And please don't pick and choose which sin you'll help with. Remember, the word says, "All have sinned and fallen short of the glory of God" (Romans 3:23). Yes, I fell short, but I should not have been neglected because of my sin. I should have not been neglected.

Chapter Twenty-Five

ORPHAN

About a month ago, at my late pastor's memorial service, one of the speakers who was giving reflections about the pastor mentioned that she and a few friends of hers felt like the orphans of the church that they came from. I then looked up the definition of an orphan: a person or thing that is without protective affiliation, sponsorship, etc. (i.e., "I lost the protection of the church"). When I heard those words, it hit me that, besides the feeling of being abandoned, I've felt like an orphan as well. Both my parents died in 1996, and I was orphaned by my first church in Fredericksville when I fell into sin. I felt as though I was left to just rot and fester, and to find my way all by myself. My pastor was too afraid of what people would think about him doing his duty as a pastor to me, being part of his flock. The elder of the church didn't assist in my spiritual life as well. I was practically begging for help, for people to still love me and, as men, be there for me and with me, but it was to no avail. No one ever wanted to leave the flock to come after the one. To me, they wanted to stay with the ninety-nine and leave the one that was lost and needed them out for the wolves to devour.

I've been a loner most of my life. I didn't trust too many people. I found out why: because, as the word says, out of the heart comes the issues of life (Proverbs 4:23). And when I was in trouble, real trouble, I truly found out who my real friends were and were not. I found through my incarceration that the pastor wasn't the man of God that I thought he was. I became an orphan of the church. I didn't have the love I needed; I didn't have the respect I needed. All I had was a bunch of people whispering here and there and not really worried about the sheep that was lost out in the world.

So now I truly understand what the definition of an orphan is: when the people that were supposed to love you leave you out on your own. But God reached way down and picked me up and said, "Kai, I love you and will never forsake you," and moved me to where He wanted me to be. I was no longer an orphan. I am now in a place of love, a place of comfort, a place I can call home. I have a church family now that cares about my every being, starting with my spiritual to what's going on in my life. They accepted me by getting to know my heart. I'm in a place that knows the true meaning of love, where they don't just say it, they show it, too.

Chapter Twenty-Six
THE MUD

Last night. as I was talking to a couple of young ladies in Panera Bread, I brought up the subject of bitterness and getting even. For some reason, I mentioned this after overhearing them talking about something on this subject. I told them that the word says a righteous man falls seven times but he gets up (Proverbs 24:16). I then went on to say something profound. I said many people will fall in the mud, and instead of getting up, washing, and moving on, they will stay in the mud, wallow in it, and expect others to feel sorry for them. But the Lord gave this to me. He said you have a choice: either you get up, clean yourself off, and then move on, or you can stay there and feel sorry for yourself, and want others to feel sorry for you as well. That's not what God wants. When men sin, he wants us to confess our sin, get up, and move forward, and not let anyone try to hold that sin over us ever again. I told them that I was going to put this in my book because I know the feeling of bitterness for others that kept trying to keep me in the mud. But Kai got up and cleaned off, just as David did after his sin, and moved forward.

Chapter Twenty-Seven

SAMANTHA JAMES, THE FRIEND WHO FOUND ME

It was the beginning of summer. On May 27, 2010, I got a message on Facebook from an old friend, Samantha James. She said for me to contact her. I was truly shocked, because I had lost contact with her a long time ago. Her girls were still little when we had last talked to each other. I contacted her on Facebook and gave her my number to call me. She texted me and I texted her back, and it went from there.

    We finally got a chance to talk and it was fun, different, and surprising. I discovered that she had found the Lord in her life and finally left her children's father. She talked about the Lord and it was refreshing to hear that. She reminded me that I used to take her to church, and about the spicy chicken incident at

Kentucky Fried Chicken, which was rather funny. I smiled and thanked the Lord for her finding me. She said she'd been looking for me for a while now. I couldn't understand why. Why, at this moment in my life, was Samantha, who I really liked after my first wife left me, looking for me? Then it hit me. The Lord used Samantha to remind me of Kai—of all the good that I used to do.

While we were talking, Sam kept asking if I was still teaching or working with kids. I kept trying to avoid the question. I told her that I was working on something else right now, but in due time I would be. We exchanged information and then started talking day by day. I told Samantha that if she came down and we went to dinner, I would tell her. She said she would, and it was a welcome reply. I cried after we got off the phone, because I have no ordinary past now, and I didn't know how she was going to react. She knew me before I fell, before I got into all this mess. How would Samantha react to a long-lost friend of hers who fell into sin and was a felon now?

June 26, 2010, finally came. A month after she found me, Samantha got on the road from Philadelphia to come see me. I was proud to see her driving, because when I left Philadelphia, she wasn't; I was driving her everywhere.

She came down, made her way to my house on Baltimore Street, and saw my transition home. And the funny thing is that she didn't mind. She had a blue jeans outfit on that was really beautiful. Samantha always had a beautiful smile, and I could see our Father in her. She let me drive, since it was my city and unfamiliar to her. We drove around, I had to run to the post office, and then I showed her the area where I used to live in Baltimore

County. After that, we went to Applebee's for dinner. I think I had the Philly steak. She had an appetizer, which was supposed to be just that, an appetizer, but Samantha ate the whole thing like it was a meal. I love seeing her eat because I know she has a hearty appetite. So, during our afternoon meal, I told her what had happened. After she heard about it, her reaction was that she knew it had something to do with children. Samantha knew that I loved teaching, and when I told her that I wasn't teaching, she knew something was wrong. But she told me that I could have told her over that phone and she still would have come. And I really appreciated those words. She knew me before all this craziness happened to me.

We then left the restaurant and drove back to my place, and were about to catch the bus to downtown Baltimore. While we were waiting we talked some more, and Samantha made a great observation. She told me that my wife had already divorced me in her heart a long time ago, and was just going through the motions now. I thought about it, and said she was right. I had never thought of it that way. It was getting late, and we decided that we wouldn't make it to the harbor to go boat riding and get back in time for her to get back on the road to Philadelphia. We got in her van and just chatted for a second. She then got herself together and headed for Philadelphia. This was the beginning of something special from a long-lost special friend. Well, I was actually the one who was lost, and God used her to find me and tell me that everything was going to be OK.

Thank you, Samantha James...

Chapter Twenty-Eight
EVERY WHICH WAY BUT RIGHT

Samantha and I were talking one morning on the phone, as we always do since we've been reconnected, and were discussing a friend and what he was going through. And she made this statement: she said he was going "every which way but right." I said, "Wow, I like that, because it reminds me of what I went through to get to where I am now." For twenty-three years I was going every which way but right. I thought everything I was doing was right in the eyes of God, but it wasn't. I was brought up in the Mennonite Church, I taught Sunday school, I was a deacon at one time, I was the minister of music—you name it, I did it. But at the age of twenty-five, after meeting my first wife, my godly life changed. The funny thing is, it wasn't a big change. It was a gradual change, to where I didn't even know the path that I set myself on.

I was a young man in college working on my BA in music education, working at McDonald's, and just trying to live life right. At the age of twenty-five, I was still a virgin who wanted that special someone, just like everyone else, and that was my Achilles' heel. I fell in love at eighteen with a young lady in church, but found out that she liked the bad boys, so there wasn't any room for me. Her mother loved me, but I had unrequited love for her.

I met Gloria at the age of twenty-five, and being a straight-up guy, tried my best to be a gentleman. We met at church because our two churches always fellowshipped together. She was a beautiful young lady with lovely eyes. I know, I've always been a sucker for beautiful eyes. Anyway, one day while I was working at McDonald's, she came to the restaurant and I was in the back. They told me that a young lady by the name of Gloria was there to see me. I said, "Gloria who?" Well, to my surprise it was the young lady from the other church. I asked her to have a seat in the lobby. I went out there with her for a minute, and she asked me nervously if I'd be her date to a banquet that her church was having. I said yes. Who wouldn't want a beautiful young lady to ask him out? You'd be crazy to say no. So I took her information, and when I got off work we talked, and later started seeing each other more often when I had time from work, church, and all the other things I was doing. I was trying to be a good Christian young man, but it was hard.

I eventually went to the banquet with her and had a great time. I would go over her house. Her room was down the basement, and I'd go down there and we'd have our private time together, which was a big mistake. We'd start kissing and hugging, and one thing would lead to another. We'd start getting horny and then it was all she wrote, no pun intended. Gloria was my first real sexual experience, and my first oral sex experience. So you know I really wanted to see her more often. I was still going to church, still going to school, still working, and still teaching Sunday school, which was all a bad mixture because I was out of His will. I was every which way but right.

Chapter Twenty-Nine
THE ANONYMOUS CALL

It was December 2010, a beautiful afternoon, and after I got off work I had to head over to the probation office in downtown Baltimore to report to my third probation officer. I signed in as usual and then caught the elevator to the third floor. I went in and signed in at the desk to see him. All was going as planned because I'd been doing this for a whole year. When it was my turn to see him, he called me into his office and asked me the strangest question. He asked if I had had any contact with the victim. I asked him why he would ask me something like that. He said that he had received an anonymous call that I did. He then proceeded to tell me that when he asked who was reporting this, the person hung up. I asked him, "Do you really think that I've come this far in my first year of probation and would do something that crazy, knowing that I have to report to you weekly?"

I told him it was probably my soon-to-be-ex-wife. That was the year I chose to stop talking to her and answering her texts, and she didn't like that I was ignoring her. That was also the year I found out that she was cheating on me with her ex-husband. So, since I wasn't playing the game she wanted to play, she chose to try to get me in trouble. You see, if I was caught anywhere near the victim, I'd have to go back to jail and finish my full ten-year sentence. That was one thing I wasn't going to jeopardize. But being the type of woman she was at that time, she decided to call and try to get me in trouble.

He proceeded to tell me that he had to ask, for his records, and to record my answer. I myself couldn't believe that she'd something like that. I hadn't done anything to her or her family. I hadn't called her, or even tried to contact her daughter. That she would actually lie about it and try to get me in trouble was unbelievable.

I explained to him that we were about to get a divorce, and she was doing all she could to get me in trouble because I was not playing the game the way she wanted me to play it. He looked at me, we talked a bit more, and then I left until my next report date.

As I was leaving the office, I was thinking to myself that it was the most evil thing that anyone could do. You would basically lie and send me back to jail because you're going through something and I'm not giving in to you or playing the game you want me to play, and you'll risk me going back to jail. I couldn't believe that. But due to my track record with parole and probation and the rules they had to follow, I was OK. They had to ask questions, and had to prove that I had contact with the victim, and there was no proof, because Keisha didn't leave a name or a number—she just hung up.

Another thought came to me. I was wondering how many other men and women have gotten into trouble because Satan got into someone and did the same thing. I know my ex-wife wasn't the only one who did something that asinine. We have to be very careful when we hold the balance of other people's lives in our hands. This would have been the second time that she had my life in her hands, and she wasn't responsible enough to be a woman of her word. This time she was just outright lying. But, as I said earlier in this book, after all the sex had stopped, and my eyes were open, I'd found out who I was really dealing with: a woman who was very bitter and angry, and never really did love me. So what should I have expected? She was just following the program.

I told Tina about it and she couldn't believe that Keisha would do something like that. But I didn't let it get me down. I actually started praying for her more, so that one day she'll get it together and won't think that I'm the enemy. I only wanted the best for her and the kids, but since I was replaced, all I could do was pray.

Chapter Thirty
JACQUELINE, THE FRIEND

Well, in January 2011, I met a beautiful new friend on Facebook. Her name was Jacqueline. And with that beautiful and lovely friend, I allowed myself to get caught up again. She had a beautiful smile and such a sweet spirit; it was refreshing and welcome after all I'd been through. I loved listening to her, talking to her; I just loved her in general. I loved her dearly as a friend. She was a breath of fresh air to me, if you understand what I am saying. But she wanted more than that: she wanted to be the next Mrs. Montgomery, in fact. So I had to slow it down with her. I told her in the beginning that after two marriages, and eighty-six days of incarceration, I had to get right with my Creator so I could do all that He was calling me to do. She sort of understood, but was still very persistent in her efforts. So I did what was best for me. I put on the brakes for a minute to keep my head straight, and focused on what God needed me to do—and that was getting back to Kai.

The way we met on Facebook was very interesting, though. I was supposed to go to church that day, but something happened. I was on Facebook, looking at her cousin's page, when I saw her beautiful smile; the smile of sweet innocence. I took the chance of contacting her, and guess what? She responded. She told me that she was on her way out of town to visit some friends, but we still texted through Facebook practically the whole day. She seemed very interested in me. I certainly was interested in her. That day was such a tragedy, but she was a beautiful ending to it. We talked for a couple of days and then something prompted me to tell her about my secret past, so I did. And by the grace of God, she understood.

After telling her, we talked more and more. We ooVoo'd, we Yahooed, we were practically inseparable, even though we were several thousand miles away from each other. She was in Texas, and I was in Maryland. But one day, the South met the North and they really fell for each other. She took my heart; she wanted to be part of my life, and she wanted to be part of my dreams. She knew that I was at the end of a marriage and the divorce was happening soon. She was a writer, too, and a great one at that. She had that kind of imagination that when she wrote, you thought the things she was writing about were really happening to you. I loved reading her love stories; they left me breathless, and made me all emotional, and just had me. She also helped me financially. Jacqueline just really cared about Kai.

A month after we met, we made plans for my Southern belle to come up. Her birthday was the next month, and I wanted her here so that we could spend time together and celebrate her day. So we made the plans: she'd fly up, rent a car, and stay in a hotel downtown. She reserved a room at the hotel on St. Paul and Fayette Streets in Baltimore, Maryland. We had room 311, which will be a room that I will always remember. She came on a Thursday and I had church that evening, so she came with me. Oh, yeah, let me back up. When she landed at Baltimore's BWI, we met, hugged, and then went to pick up the rental car. With her working for Quickie Car Rental there wasn't much of a problem, but they didn't have the car she asked for in stock, so they upgraded us to a Blue Ford Edge, which I fell in love with. She let me do all the driving since it was my city and she was the guest. So, yeah, we went church, and it was a great service. I introduced her to our elder's wife and a few others, and she was able to see me sing with the choir. After the service, we went to my best friend's house (where I was staying) to get my things, and then went back to the hotel.

Now, once we got back and were settled in, we got some food together and turned on the television. And then we had a moment where we looked into each other's eyes. I just grabbed her, and started caressing her, rubbing my hands all over her beautiful face, and kissing her sweet lips. We kissed like there was no tomorrow, and made sweet passionate love. We ate, talked, and fell asleep in each other's arms because I had to go to work the next day.

I got up the next morning, showered, and got ready for work. I went downstairs and got her breakfast so that she wouldn't have to. I then went to the parking lot, got in the truck, and went to work. I checked on her all day while I was at work.

She was in the room chilling or watching television; she was fine. She stayed about a week. She got me some things when she went shopping. I wasn't even expecting it; I thought she was going shopping for herself, and she ended up coming back with things for me. She went to Sunday service with me, and had a great time. We celebrated her birthday that weekend. It wasn't what she thought it was going to be, but that was my fault. I had too many things that I was trying to get done that weekend. I think the other reason was because I had to work as well, and that didn't leave a lot of room and time for an out-of-town guest.

It was a week to remember. We learned more about each other; yes, we made more sweet passionate love that was a totally memorable experience. The week went by fast, and I didn't want her to leave. You see, when you're lonely, it's hard to have a short experience like that and then it ends. But she had to leave. She made plans for the shuttle to pick her up from the hotel. I kissed her that Thursday morning, and then took the truck to work.

POEM
STAY THE COURSE

We all have a past that the world doesn't want to forget,
We all have a future that Satan tries his best to upset,
We've done things that we're sorry for,
We wish we could go back and change the score.

But knowing now that Jesus came and wiped my sins away,
I don't have to continue to listen to what others have to say,
They try to hold me to that ever-forgetful past,
But Jesus said, my son, your sins are gone at last.

I was told just the other day that you have to stay the course,
I was told the other day that my God-ordained purpose
will be a great and mighty force,
I was told the other day that my Christian position
will not be liked,
But as He told Joshua, don't look left or right.
To keep my eyes on the one and only prize,
which is Jesus Christ.

There is a purpose for what's going on in my life,
The winds are blowing around me with a mighty strife.
I've been called what the word says is a pestilence.
But I'm OK with that, 'cause I know I have to stay the course,
That is the thing I chose as my defense, to stay the course.

Written: April 2011

Chapter Thirty-One
THE EX-HUSBAND, THE AFFAIR

The first time Keisha told me that she had an affair with her ex-husband, I couldn't believe it. The way she told me was like, I did it and that's that. She even tried to blame it on me. You see, how I found out was like this.

My wife had to wake up early every morning because she worked in Columbia, Maryland, so she needed time to get there. She loved her sleep. Well, one Friday evening while I was still in my transitional home, she called my cell and asked me for her PIN number to her card. Now, I didn't pay this any mind because it was not an unusual request. But when I woke up, I thought about it, and then I called and asked her, "What were you doing out after eleven p.m.?" When I heard her answer—even I didn't think she was bold enough to say it—she said she was with her children's father. I asked her, "Well, what were you guys doing?" And she said, "Doing what grown folks do." Now, being me, and not expecting this from her, I said, "And what is that?" And she said, "We had a rendezvous." And after hearing that, it clicked, and the adrenaline immediately rushed to my head, and I asked her, "Were you and him having sex?" And she said, "Yes." Mind you, this was a month after I was released, and she and I had had sex as well.

I hung up the phone and then had to get out of the house. I had some things to do and then I treated myself to a movie. I turned my phone off so that she couldn't contact me. I needed to clear my head, and have some me time, and not worry about her foolishness. After the movie ended, I turned my phone back on and there were texts from her. I caught my bus, went home, and just chilled because I really didn't want to talk to her. The next day was Sunday and I went to church. She called me as I was in Sunday school and I decided to talk to her. I went out of the sanctuary and talked to her in the hallway. She asked if I was all right. I told her I was fine, I just needed time to think about what was going on. She then asked if we could meet and talk. I agreed to that, and made a date to meet her in a couple of days.

She came over to my place, and as always, I tried to at least continue to be a husband and be nice to her. We went up to my room to talk, and she began to tell me that she and her ex were talking about what had happened between her daughter and me, and then one thing led to another and they ended up having sex. But I noticed that while she was talking to me, she was not able to look me in the eye. Her head was turned to the side as she was talking. That was a clue that she was lying. So I said to her, "You're trying to tell me that it was my fault that you and your children's father started sleeping together that evening." She said yes. And then I was thinking, *Does she really hear what she's saying?*

So, being me, I forgave her, and then proceeded to try to make up. But you have to remember, just a few days ago she slept with another man, and then we were trying to make up. I had a confusing, soap-opera-type feeling going on in my head. I was feeling like I was playing a starring role in a movie and that I was the one being walked on. You see, she didn't realize what she was doing, or at least I didn't think she did. When we first met, she told me that they were divorced because he had cheated on her, and there she was doing the exact same thing with the man that had done it to her. I couldn't even fathom that ever happening, but it did. She became just what he had been, an adulterer, and she liked it. I'd come to the conclusion that she divorced him on paper, but never in her heart.

As time went on, I eventually found out that that wasn't the first night they had been together—it had been many times before, and even while I was incarcerated. I found out a long time ago that whatever is done in the dark eventually is shown in the light.

One night in April 2010, as I was asleep in my house, something had me get up in the middle of the night and go on the Internet. I did, and something told me to log on to the Sprint Picture Mail that my wife and I shared. I got on, and to my unfortunate surprise, I saw explicit pictures of her that she was sending to some man. Mind you, she was on vacation with her sister, which I helped pay for, and I had rented a car for her as well with some of my unemployment funds. As I was looking at these pictures, one was of a message that she wrote in the sand that read: "I love you, Terrance." Then I saw pictures of her body parts that she sent to him. Well, we all know that I was truly shocked. The cat was out the bag. I called her and immediately she started lying, asking why I was all up on her stuff. She forgot that we shared that account, and that I was helping with paying the bill, and was always calling for extensions so that she and the kids would have phones.

I don't know what made me get up that evening, because I normally don't get up to check the picture mail, but I got up and the truth came out. The only thing I can think of is that the Holy Spirit woke me up and made me sign on so that I could see the truth, and to prepare me for anything that would come after that.

I called her the next morning as she was on her way back home after leaving the airport. She said to me in a small voice, "You know what it's time for," meaning it was time for a divorce. When she got back, we didn't talk for a few days because it was marinating in my mind. I kept going to work, but I was going through hell mentally, and would cry here and there, getting it all out of my system. I couldn't believe she was lying to me the whole time. I felt icky because she was having sex with him and with me. Lying to me, telling me that her vagina hurt because of an infection, and the whole time it was because she was doing all kinds of kinky and crazy stuff with him.

The Friday after discovering what was going on, everything I had learned, and read, was put to the test. After work, I went to talk to my best friend for a minute; I then went to the store to pick up a few things. And as I was walking up and down the street, I was crying like nothing in this world. I was thinking about him, I was thinking about her, I was thinking that I was not going out like that. I'd already dealt with the hurt of what I did to my stepdaughter, and now she was making me have to deal with this. I was crying left and right and didn't know what to do.

I went back to the house and to my room to watch TV, and then something happened. As I was watching TV my heart started racing, my breathing got heavy, and it felt like I was having a heart attack. I didn't like the way I was feeling; I had to give this some attention or else. The hospital was only four blocks away, but I didn't want to go because I knew what this was. For the first time in my life, at the age of forty-six, I was having an anxiety attack. I didn't know what to do about it, so I started looking online for the answer. Eventually, I found a solution online and started doing it immediately. I opened the front door so I could get some air. It was bitterly cold that evening, too, but I didn't care—I needed some air. I needed to get myself together so this thing wouldn't take me out, as it was trying to. I even tried calling my best friend for help, but there wasn't anyone available that evening, no one but God. I prayed, got up and went for a walk around the block, went back in, got myself ready for bed, and then went to sleep.

When I woke up the next morning, I called my best friend and told her what had happened. She was in shock, and apologized for not being available. I told her there was no need; I know she has a husband and family and won't always be available. I got over it and was deep in thought that whole day. When Sunday came, I got up, dressed, and went to church. I immediately went to the elder and told him that I was under attack, and that I needed prayer. He didn't think twice; he didn't even hesitate. He took me downstairs to one of the Sunday school rooms and got more men together, twelve in all, and they grouped around me and began to pray for me. I cried while they were praying, and I let everything go that was bothering me. While I was letting everything out, God was pouring into me and renewing me at the same time.

After prayer, I was better. We got ready and went up to prepare for the service. I had a great service, too. I then went home and chilled again, waiting for Monday to come. When it came, I was ready to call my wife and explain to her what had happened. She said, "Yes, that was an anxiety attack, and now you know how I feel." And I asked her, "Is this what it's all about? Trying to get even because of what I did?" She couldn't answer me, so at that point, in the back of my head, I knew I had to do it. Now was the time to get a divorce. You see, in the three years before all this happened, she'd always threaten me to get the divorce, but it never surfaced. But now I was going to get it because I'd decided to love Kai more than I loved her. I already had the information that I could get one for seventy-five dollars. I got this from a friend at work. That Friday after it all happened, I woke up and confirmed to myself that I was getting this divorce.

When I told her that, she was in agreement, and I started the procedure. In the past couple of months I'd been practically begging for sex from my own wife, not knowing that she had been sleeping with her ex-husband. So again, I decided I was better than that and didn't have to beg her for sex. I decided that I was going to be celibate and stop having sex altogether. I stopped calling her, I stopped texting her, and I began my detox from a woman that was poisoning me and my spirit. When she would call, I wouldn't answer; when she texted me, I wouldn't answer. I was going through the weaning process so that I was able to fall in love with me again and get back to the Kai I was before all this happened.

As the months went by, she was still calling and texting. We had a small war about a mirror of hers that I had in storage, and I finally decided to give it to her because it was the right thing to do. I was a little upset because it seemed as though I was the only one doing right. She would mention things that were going on between her and her ex, and some of those things she was going through with him hurt me. *I'm married to you, your ex is treating you wrong, and I can't do anything about it because you told me that you're in love with him.* She never realized that the part of me that loved her was hurting because he was treating her like trash. But because of her self-centeredness, it went right over her head. That was one of the things I had to get through, being in love with someone who didn't love me, who loved another man. It wasn't the easiest thing to get through, but God knew, and He was there and ready for me.

I remember one Friday evening she called rather late and wanted me to talk to her because the children's father wasn't picking up his phone. He was at home with his wife. She had to take the baby boy and some of his friends to the movies. She was tired and cold, but she took them anyway. The theater they went to was on the other side of Baltimore, so she drove them, and had to wait while they went to the movie. The kid's father could have taken them because he lives on that side, but he didn't. He stayed in and didn't answer the phone because he was at home with his own wife. And my wife, for some reason, felt that she was more important, and wanted him to come out, instead of her waiting alone in a dark parking lot. He didn't care. I did, but couldn't do anything about it.

I kept her company on the phone for a little while, then let her go. I'd come to the conclusion that if you're grown, and make decisions that aren't really healthy for you, and choose not to listen to wisdom, then you'll have to reap what you sow. I loved her, but this was out of my hands, and I had to learn to live with that. She never knew that when he treated her wrong, he was treating me wrong, and I couldn't do anything about it but deal with it.

Chapter Thirty-Two

'TIS BETTER TO HAVE LOVED AND LOST THAN NEVER TO HAVE LOVED AT ALL

This thought came to me at the end of my marriage to my second wife. Before I went into BDF for my eighty-six-day stay in the fall of 2009, she and I were finally falling in love. Yes, that's what I said, we were falling in love. You see, for our first date of a *Spider-Man* movie and a pizza, she came over to my apartment. I was surprised that she found it, but she did. I had recently kicked out my ex-girlfriend and hadn't had sex in a while. So I was vulnerable and didn't even realize it. When she came over, she was looking real sexy. Scoping out my apartment, she bent over to check out my CD collection. As I watched her bend over, I saw her sweet pink thong, and that piqued my interest. I thought to myself, *Wow, she has a pink thong on.* She sat on the love seat as I sat on the big couch. I got her some pizza, turned on the movie, and we watched it for a minute. We made some small talk for a minute, too. I then asked her to sit next to me. She did. I put my arms around her and we continued to watch the movie.

Then it was time to make my move. I bent over to kiss her and she kissed me, and it felt good. Remember now, I haven't had any intimacy with a woman since my ex, Asia, and I broke up the month before and I kicked her out. So we kissed, and I love kissing. I started caressing her body, and she caressed mine, and you know what happened after that, right? Yes, I went and got a condom and we had sex, and it was good. We were totally compatible, more than with anyone I'd ever been with. But here's the side bar: how many times will God allow Satan to bring something to you, and make it really appealing to you, knowing it's going to have you all caught up? As many times as it takes for us to finally say no, not bend, not fall, and to trust in Him, and obey Him fully and completely. Well, I wasn't there yet, so a partner was allowed into my life that I was so compatible with sexually that every time we had sex, or made love, it was always good. The date ended and she went home. We started talking on the phone, as all people who think they're in love do, and it was on since then.

The next morning, I had to wake up, get ready for church, and go play the piano as the assistant to the minister of music at my church. Now, think about it, I was a leader in the church, up at the piano, and the night before I was having sex with one of the members in my apartment. As I think of it now, I know why I felt the way I did that morning. Did anyone know? Did they suspect anything? I didn't know at that moment that my ministry was going to be taken away from me because once again I had given in to my weakness, instead of trusting and obeying God, and this time I was going to have to learn it the hard way.

So there I was again, thinking I was falling in love with this person, when all the time I was falling in lust with her. Her body was all that, she was good in bed, we were very compatible, but we were out of the will of God. We were in the church, but we were wrong. We were not being good examples to her children. I have worked with kids my whole life and I valued that part of me, and I let them down. I didn't let just them down; I let God down by taking my life into my own hands instead of trusting it in His. I should have been a better example to my new girlfriend and her children, but I got caught up in it all.

I thought I was falling in love, but I wasn't—I was in lust. By the middle of the year I was ready to marry her because I didn't want to sleep with anyone else and didn't want her to sleep with anyone else as well. So we started making arrangements to get married. I was teaching at a local Baltimore school and making good money. We had met in 2004, right after I got that new teaching gig, and it was actually pretty convenient to have a new job, a new girl, and a better paycheck. But again, it was still wrong. I wasn't being the example I should have been for her or her children. I knew it was wrong, but the false feeling I was getting from all the sex and lust was messing up my sensors. She did join the church, started singing in the choir, and we were actually becoming a good couple together, but we were secretly doing things we should not have been doing.

That summer the pastor bought a new church van and was looking for a driver to pick up church members who needed transportation. For some reason he thought I wanted to do it. He didn't know I had done that before at my old church back home in Philadelphia, and even the thrill of that wore off, but I did it to be obedient. Then he had the nerve to ask her to go with me, to help guide me around the city because he knew that I didn't know Baltimore that well. I felt some kind of way about that, but didn't realize it gave us a chance to start spending more time together. I'd pick up the van from the church, pick her up, and then we would pick up other members. So it actually was a good thing. She started showing me her skills for knowing how to get around Baltimore. I eventually started calling her my MapQuest.

After I started working my music teacher gig at the school, I started meeting new teachers. We kept dating, and I was learning more and more about her. But one day, out of nowhere, she told me that she didn't want to see me anymore. I asked her why, but she didn't want to give me an answer. Since we had just met, I wasn't really stressed about, and being me, I decided, *Hey, I don't want to be alone tonight*, so I reached out to a friend that I'd known before her, Tammy. I asked her to come over and spend some time with me. I got some Chinese food and she came over. Tammy was a good friend, and I'd been trying to be alone with her for a minute, but it never happened. So the moment I had her alone—we were watching television in my room and eating Chinese food—I heard a knock at the door.

I went to the door, and lo and behold, it was Keisha, my new ex-girlfriend. I couldn't believe it. I peeped out the door and asked what she was doing there. I didn't want to let her in because that meant she was going to see my guest. But she pushed in and I immediately could tell that she was under the influence of her medication. She was wondering why I didn't want to let her in, so she eventually went into the bedroom and acted like a crazy, foolish woman. She scared Tammy away, and I was as embarrassed as could be. She was getting on me, saying that I had someone in her spot on my bed. I told her that she got rid of me, and I was just having a friend over, but she didn't want to hear that. She thought everything was about sex, and that I was trying to have sex with Tammy.

I'm not one who likes drama, and that was what happened that evening. I'd never had this kind of stuff in my life and didn't know where it was coming from. I know now where it came from; it came from the medication she was taking. Even though it made her drowsy, she always drove when she was under the influence of that medication. But again, I wasn't a drama type of person. If you say that you don't want me, then you don't want me. At the time, I didn't know that was a sign for me to stay out of a relationship with her, and I didn't.

The funny thing is that she went to church the next day, and afterward started telling the other women at the church about it and they took her side. Again, if you tell someone you don't want to see him anymore, don't lie about it to play games, just tell the truth: you want him or you don't. So I had to take the harassment from the other women at the church. Oddly, I was at that church longer than her or her mother, who was an evangelist, but everyone seemed to take their side about everything.

So we got back together in order to try it again. I didn't think anything more about that situation. I'm the type of person who thinks what happened has happened, and I can't go back to fix it; all I can do is move on. We started getting closer again, still having sex outside marriage. Her kids were learning more about me and I was having fun with them. We were really starting to look like a family. She and I were having sex like bunny rabbits all the time, anytime of day we wanted because we were that compatible, and I always pleased her and she always pleased me. Now, side bar: how many of us know that right there was a setup? And the other fact was that she had had her tubes tied, so I didn't have to worry about her having more children. Again, everything that looks good isn't always good for you.

So, being me, thinking that I was in love because she did anything and everything I wanted when it came to sex, I decided I wanted to marry her. Not thinking with the right head, as we say. Since she was living in her own place, paying two sets of bills was too much work on us financially, so we decided to move in together. How many of us already know that was wrong, too? I again was conforming to my standards and the world's view, and not God's. The world says you don't have to get married, that living together is enough, but in God's sight that's totally wrong. So again, for the second time in my life, I moved a woman into my home.

I didn't even think of how the children would feel, or how it looked to them. God knew I wanted a family, He put it in me, but He also knew that I wanted a family so badly that I'd do anything to get it, and that's just what I did. I did anything. I should have been the leader and said, "Let's not do it this way. Let's wait and do it right." Children are so impressionable, and I was doing all the wrong things right in front of them. They needed a leader in their life who loved God and was willing to wait for the right time to do what was best for them, and God. But I didn't do that. I conformed for sex and out of my own wants, needs, and desires. I wanted their mother close in case I wanted her or she wanted me.

Then the inevitable happened. The pastor found out and called us into his office. He brought us before the elder and the others, and asked if we were living together. We told him yes, and gave him the reason why. The reason was that we were going to get married; we just wanted to save money by living together before the wedding date. He said that since I was a leader in the church as the church musician, I couldn't do that; if it was found out, it would cause chaos. He said, "Either she moves out, or you get married." So what did we do? We got married in the summer of 2005, a year after we first met. We were trying to wait till February 2006, but instead, we got married because of what the pastor said, and to make it right. We went to the justice of the peace in Towson, Maryland, one midafternoon, got married, and went back to work. The ceremony lasted only three minutes,

I kid you not. When we came out, the next couple looked at us as if surprised and we gave them that look like yes, we were shocked, too. So that action was right, but the intention and motive were wrong. We only got married because we wanted to continue to have sex legally. We truly didn't know each other and weren't ready.

Chapter Thirty-Three
THE DIVORCE

I went to the divorce hearing on the second of March, 2011, and when I got there I was stunned that she brought her daughter with her. I was surprised because she knew there was a court order stating I couldn't be anywhere near her or I'd be out of compliance with my probation. She knew this, so why would she bring her there, I wondered. But I guess the Lord knew what she was up to. She brought a couple of things to the master's attention, like money owed to the attorney for working on my case, and the master said that was between her and the lawyer. She got her name back, and we signed the papers so that we wouldn't have to wait to go in front of a judge. I then received a letter stating that I owed the court $130.00 for court fees, but after talking to the people that helped me with the paperwork, we finally got it done. So as of last week, the week of May 9, 2011, we were officially divorced. When I received the official divorce decree I did get emotional and cried a little, because I had buried another marriage and had to deal with it.

God has brought me a long way, and I thank Him for helping me through it because I know I couldn't have done it without His help. He showed me how to love myself first before I could learn to love anyone else. Unconditional love is a love that our world really doesn't know. We think we're in love with that person, when all we really are is in lust with that person. I knew this, because when trouble started heading our way, my ex-wife told me that she only married me because the sex was good. But thanks be unto God; He used her to teach me what unconditional love is. That's the kind of love that Christ had for the Father and us when He went to the cross for our sins. A man must love his wife as Christ loved the church.

Chapter Thirty-Four
REFLECTION OF MARRIAGE

On August 5, 2011, I suddenly began reflecting on my marriage life. I think it was after August 4 came, and I told my manager at work it would have been twenty-one years of marriage to my first wife if I had stayed married to her. But she left me in 1999, after nine years of marriage. The divorce wasn't finalized until June or July 2005. That means we were legally married for fifteen years. I then had girlfriends and was out of the will of God, fornicating left and right, trying to find someone to love me for me, still keeping one foot in the church and not knowing that I was being set up.

I met my first real girlfriend in Philadelphia the summer after my first wife left. I met Asia on the Internet—on Black Planet, if I remember correctly—in the summer of 2000. We chatted on AOL and decided to meet in public to be safe. We met at a diner on Grant Avenue in Northeast Philadelphia, ate, and then went to see a movie. We hit it off right away. After a while of talking, she came over one day to my house on Bailey

Street in Philadelphia, and brought one of her boys who was an infant. After putting the baby to sleep, we started kissing in the kitchen and one thing led to another. We ended up having sex and it was great. She had the sweetest lips I've ever kissed, and the sex was phenomenal. She then left and went back to her mother's place, and we kept in contact after that.

We would go out and then go back to my place. One night, the sex was so great that she said she wanted to have my baby. I fell in love with her because I was able to give myself wholly to her. But during that summer, she decided to move back to Baltimore because she needed a new full-time job and found one there. So she packed up and moved. We tried the long-distance thing for a minute, but it got slow and I missed her.

In November of that same year, when I was substitute teaching in Camden, I decided to spend Thanksgiving with my brother who was living in Baltimore with my aunt Elizabeth. So I did, and while there, I decided for some reason to go and look for a job. Lo and behold, Baltimore County was hiring and looking for a music teacher. I started the paperwork and was immediately set up for an interview.

So, after a few months of going back and forth to Baltimore on Greyhound, I got the job. I decided to move; leave the house and take a leap of faith and go. Asia did ask me if I was sure that I wanted to move and leave everything behind, and I told her yes. Both my parents had died in 1996 and I didn't have anything left. My wife had left me, my parents were gone, and my brother was already in Baltimore. So I moved to Baltimore, Maryland. The only people I knew were my family and Asia and her two babies. But I made it work so that I could move on with my life.

The relationship between Asia and me started being on and off because she was still trying to find herself. Asia was thirteen years younger than me, and was going through some things in her life as well. She loved me as I loved her, but family issues were keeping her from loving me completely, I think, the way she wanted to. Asia knew there wasn't anything I wouldn't do for her. After moving back to Baltimore, Asia eventually lost her apartment because the bills were more than she could handle at that time, and she lost that job, too. So, being me, I said she could move in with me. Again, I was breaking one of my rules. I'd never let a woman move in with me, but I was compromising my morals for the love of a woman. I was now a musician in a church. I really didn't want to play for another church because I'd done that for almost twenty years of my life and wanted to retire. But eventually the itch came back and I needed to play.

So there I was again, playing for a church and a choir, and having a woman I was not married to living with me. Well, eventually things got crazy between Asia and me and I got tired of her living with me, especially since it was now 2004 and I was going through a job problem and financial problems, and she did not want to grow up and help. So in the summer of 2004 I put her out. My friends didn't think I was going to do it, but I did. I had to do it; it was too much. I loved her, but had to love me more.

That same summer, right after I put her out, I met Keisha, my soon-to-be second wife. And like with the first wife, the same thing happened; we met, had a date, and started having sex. The sex was great, and we were very compatible with each other. But I knew deep down inside it was wrong. I was still the church musician, and I was fornicating.

I was supposed to be an example to the youth, and waiting for love, but instead, I was letting them down, I was letting my pastor down, and, most importantly, I was letting God down. She was a church member, but we got caught up in the sex. Since everything was good on that end, I thought we were in love, and I wanted to marry her after just a few months of dating, having sex, and her buying me things. She did things with me sexually that no other woman had done, and it was good—I mean, real good. But we all know that it was a ploy of the devil to keep me distracted from the mission I was running from.

While dating her I saw some strange signs that I'd never seen before in a woman. She was depressed at times; she told me about her migraines and the medication she would take to control them. She said the medicine would make her drowsy. One time when she was depressed she wrote me a suicide letter, telling me that I would be better off without her. She even stopped seeing me for a second because of that. She said she didn't want to see me anymore. I then got a date for that Saturday evening. I called Tammy; mind you, I'd had a crush on Tammy for a long time, ever since I'd been in Baltimore. I taught her little sister in Northwest Academy, and had always wanted to have a date with her. We'd talked here and there, and I'd even tried giving her guitar lessons, and taught piano to one of her daughters.

So I finally got a chance to have a date with her. I called her, we met, went and got Chinese food, returned to my apartment, and chilled in my bedroom to watch movies as we ate dinner. Well, to my surprise, Keisha came over, knocking on my door. I peeped through the peephole and was surprised it was her. I tried to open the door a little bit to ask why she was there. She busted in and was asking what was going on. I could tell she had taken her medication because she was drowsy. She eventually made it to my bedroom and basically scared my guest so badly that she ran. I couldn't believe it; this woman had made a mess of my evening and I felt like I was living in a soap opera. So you see, she said she didn't want to see me again, I decided to have a date, and then she came back, started all this drama, and scared off someone who was inside my home. If I had been thinking then, I would have realized that was a sign, but I didn't.

Chapter Thirty-Five
FORGIVING MYSELF

Forgiveness is a very hard thing when you've fallen into sin. When it was discovered that I had hurt my stepdaughter, I was blown away. It was something that I knew was wrong, I tried to stop it, I got caught up in it, and it blew up in my face. It was out then; the pastor knew, my best friend knew, and I had hurt the ones I was supposed to protect from others. I was at the lowest point in my life. You see, people think about the person that was hurt, but if you had known me, you would have seen that I was hurting, too. I'm a perfectionist; I pride myself on doing what's right. But I fell, not thinking that I could, or that it was even possible to fall. I had all the pride in the world and I needed to be humbled, and this experience did just that.

You see, this sin of mine hurt the deepest part of me. It hurt my relationship with my family, and with my church, and, more than anything, my relationship with God. I was not only worried about trying to fix it, trying to make it right, but trying to keep my sanity in the process.

At that time, I didn't know how to forgive myself. I wanted to commit suicide, I wanted to end it. I lost the things in life that I loved. I lost what I was. I hurt the people I loved. I didn't know what to do. I didn't know where to go. I just drove around many days looking for answers, being separated from my wife. She was going to counseling with me and trying to help me figure out why. I wanted forgiveness from others, I wanted forgiveness from the church, I wanted forgiveness from God, but I didn't know how to forgive myself. I looked online and found a Charles Stanley PDF file titles: "How to Forgive Yourself." I read it and it enlightened me. I really needed that, because at that moment it felt as if everyone had turned their backs on me. Sure, my wife was trying her best to be there for me, but there were a lot of questions still in her mind, like why? I could never tell her, because I didn't know. But that pamphlet on forgiving yourself really helped me. God took that burden off me and I forgave myself. The feeling of wanting to commit suicide slowly left me, and gave me an urgency to get closer to God.

When David sinned and a baby was conceived from the adultery between him and Bathsheba, he cried before God, and fasted to plead for the baby's life. But when the baby died, he got up, cleaned up, and went about his business. His servants didn't know how to accept that, but he told them that God did what he did and he had to accept it (2 Samuel 11:1–12:23). And even after the adultery, the murder, David was still known as a man after God's own heart. David knew that God forgave him, but he still had to suffer his punishment for his sins. I read that and understood immediately that I was going to go through trials, but God would always be with me and would never leave me.

Chapter Thirty-Six
A LETTER TO MY MOTHER

Dear Twinkie,

It's been a while since I really thought about you or have even written to you since the day you left this earth to be with our Heavenly Father. The last time I saw you with your eyes open will always be a day I will never forget. I do thank God that I took the time to go to the hospital and see you, because I know I've always been busy and when you needed me I wasn't there. There were times that you left a message saying, "Kai, call your mother," and I just didn't do it like I should have. And then, when I found out that the cancer had come back, I believed in my heart that you were trying to tell me, but I just wasn't listening, and for that I am sorry. I helped you fight the first battle and I thought we were done. I didn't know it had come back until it was too late and we couldn't talk about it. I've always lived my life trying to do right by you and for you, but this was one thing I couldn't fix. I've always tried to fix things when it came to you, but for the first time in my life I couldn't fix it. It was totally out of my hands.

I was going through so much with the things that were happening in my marriage, plus working and trying to get an education. I didn't get to know my own mother like I should have. We had the first ten years of our lives together, and then we were separated, to the point where we couldn't be the mother and son that we needed to be in life. I've never stopped loving you because you were the mother that God gave me, and I was the son that God gave you.

It's hard for me today, because when I need a mother, I don't have one. I get very jealous of my friends who are around the same age as me and still have their parents. Many times I have questioned God, asking Him why He took you away from me and left me alone and abandoned. This is the most hurtful feeling around, being alone and abandoned.

But knowing that you're home in Heaven with God, I plan to meet you one day. I have always appreciated Evangelist Curtis for visiting you in hospice that Friday evening before you went home with your Daddy, for witnessing to you and helping you into the Kingdom. It was one of the most important things that she did.

I know that you've always had faith in me and knew I was going to be OK, but I just wanted you to be around a little longer, so we could get it right together. But time wasn't on our side. Many days I think about you, and how we could be doing a lot of things together today, but again, time wasn't on our side. I know I hurt you when I got locked up, because I'd never been in that kind of trouble before, not until I started dating and doing things I shouldn't have. I was your baby boy who stayed out of trouble, but in my first marriage I got hooked up with the wrong person in my life, and for that I'm sorry. You had to put out money that I didn't want you to have to put out. You've seen your baby go through things that no mother should have to see after raising her children right.

I cried when you left because God gave me a gift that you never had a chance to see or hear. I've been playing the piano since the age of ten, and you never heard me. Life passed us by and we couldn't catch up. If you were alive now I'd play for you every day if I could. I want you to know that I worked hard all those years in school to make you proud of me, but again, time wasn't on our side, and I'm sorry.

I got in trouble these past few years in my second marriage and ended up incarcerated for eighty-six days for hurting a child. I know you wouldn't have wanted that to happen, but being my mother, you know my heart and would have understood. I would never want to hurt you in that way. But it happened. I didn't have anyone on my side when I was in jail, no one to love me like a mother would. I thought my wife loved me, but she didn't; I thought my pastor loved me, but he didn't. I was totally alone. But God was with me, and I learned that He was all I needed.

He gave me a calling on my life to preach the word, to be the man of God that He wants me to be, and to follow Him. But Twinkie, I'm sorry for letting you down, because I am your son, and you are my mother, and I know you would have been there for me. But this one I had to do alone so I could learn to trust God, and only Him.

I know you're happy now because Jeffery and I have found each other, and that was something only God could've done. Though each of us was trying to find the other throughout the past three years, only God could do it. That was a miracle of our life. He had us go through 2009 with tragedies and come out on top with people that love us and are there for us. Each of our best friends was there and I thank God for that. His best friend, Terry, took him in after he lost his job and was very sick. He's been living with him for the past two years. After I messed up and later got out of jail, my best friend, Tina, helped me to transition back into the world. She's been there all the time and I truly appreciate her for it.

I just wish we had had more time to get this thing called life right, but we didn't, and I've learned slowly over the years to accept that. I had you for only a short time as my mother, a spoiler, and a person I needed when times were rough, and then you were gone. I didn't even see it coming. I feel as though I made sure you were OK the first time, and then in a flash you were gone. There are many days that I cry for you, wanting to hear your voice, wanting you to listen to me play, wanting you to be my support, but you're not here. If I could do it all over again, I would do it differently; I would answer your phone calls, call you back, and even visit you more often. I just didn't know. You were trying to tell me, but I just didn't take the hints or listen. I didn't know the cancer had come back until you were dying from it.

I'm sorry my life is different now. I have a felony on my record. But the Lord our God has told me this is not the end.

I'm not letting that stop me from moving on with my life. I have dreams, and I know you would love them, too. I have worked with a young man this past year who's a fantastic musician and I've poured a lot of me into him. He plays the trumpet and I've taught him the piano. I'm going to make him one the best musicians of the future. You would be proud of me. Yes, I messed up, but God, through His help, is slowly turning things around in my favor. I love Him for that. Twinkie, I will forever love and miss you, and I will see you one day with our Heavenly Father.

Your Loving Baby Boy,
Kai

Chapter Thirty-Seven
ABANDONED

When I reflect back on my incarceration in BDF, I remember the people that abandoned me. I truly would have expected my pastor of more than seven years to have been there for me, but he abandoned me because he didn't want his name in anything. I wrote him, asked him to bail me out, and asked for money to get some underwear. I wrote him to come see me, and it was to no avail. I will never understand that. To me, it was abandonment.

My wife abandoned me to her ex-husband. She got caught up with him because of money and finances, and he used her and turned her against me. She fell in love with him for everything he's done for her and the kids while I was incarcerated. I never knew what was going on, but everything she said was going to happen with me didn't because of her being caught up with him. She forgot her vow to me as a husband. She abandoned me, took him out of the system and put me in the system, and I have a lifelong sentence in the system. It's hard right now, now that I have to deal with the registry every three months of my life, while she let me get away for sixteen thousand dollars in back child support. You see, she abandoned me for him and I will never understand that. The only thing I can think of is that she never stopped loving him, and when the opportunity arose, he came in and took advantage of her, and she forgot that she was working on getting me out with no charges. But deep down inside, I feel that he had something to do with it.

I now know how Jesus felt at the moment when He was abandoned by the disciples and had to bear His cross alone. When the people you love turn on you, it's the most hurtful feeling in the world. You do recover from it, and I did, with the help of Jesus and the Holy Spirit. I had to learn not to put my trust in people because they will fail you all the time. True friends are those that will be there even when the times are rough. I just don't want to ever go through anything like that again. The very ones that I thought would be there for me weren't, and now I know what true friendship is. I don't take friendship lightly anymore, because deep down inside I know that everyone is not my friend.

Chapter Thirty-Eight
THE FILTER

From the past few experiences I've had trying to make new friends with women today, I recently realized that I have a filter that God allowed in my life to keep me from making the same mistakes and to find out what kind of people I'm dealing with, or trying to deal with. You see, in this year of 2012, I lost four young ladies that I tried to get to know due to them finding out that I was on the registry, before I had a chance to get to know them or them to know me. The hardest thing for me is that when I'm trying to get to know people, they just shut me off completely and kick me to the curb.

There were two in the beginning of the year and two at the end of the year. Then God made me look up the definition of filter, and it is: to remove or separate by the action of a filter. You see, God has told me that this registration is my filter. He's filtering out all the young ladies that I don't need in my life. If they are shallow or self-centered, then they don't need to be in my life. I remember telling Him that I need someone in my life who will accept me and my past, and will understand me and love me for my heart. So this man-made filter is just what I needed.

I'm a man of God who loves God and thanks Him for everything that He's done for me. I'm forever embracing this registry now. God told me that I won't be part of this for the rest of my life, so right now, as I'm embracing it, I'm learning from it, too. I have my family and best friends, and my church family who love me, and that's all I need. God is going to bring all this to pass and I'm going to continue to trust him. And for all those women who dissed me this past year, thank you. You don't know what you've given up, but I'm sure one day you'll figure it out.

Chapter Thirty-Nine

THE TWO HARDEST TRIALS IN MY LIFE

When I thought about this chapter, I really had to think it through. I thought sixteen and a half years ago, when my mother passed, that that was the hardest thing in my life I had to endure. I was also told by my first wife's best friend, who's from the islands, that when a man buries his mother, he's grown now. As I've been going through life I've been through some things, but I've always thought that nothing would get to me because of that one experience of burying my mother. I've also been jealous of my friends whose mother and fathers are still alive. You see, I lost my mom when I was going through life's struggles. I needed a parent for support. But did Kai have it? No. As always, I had to go it alone.

I don't think anyone has ever known how I felt for the past sixteen and a half years of my life. I've been trying to do everything right, trying to get ahead. I've had struggles, and was alone. No mother around for support, or even a father, because he passed the same year. That was the hardest thing for me to do. I didn't cry the whole time that I was preparing for her funeral the week of August 12, 1996. I had to be strong and take care of the arrangements, and also keep a job. But when the day of her funeral came I couldn't hold it in any longer. The tears came pouring down during the service. You see, I was about to say my last good-byes to my mother. I was about to close the casket and never see her again. She looked real good; I picked out the dress and everything with the help of Gloria, my first wife, and made sure she looked good and went out in style. One of my good friends that I worked with at that time played the piano so that I didn't have to worry about it. All I did was get the choir ready and he did the rest. So you see, that was the hardest thing I thought I would ever go through, because I had to say my last good-bye to my mother, the one who carried me for nine months, and the one who tried all her life to be there. Yes, she wasn't perfect, but she did her best, and that's all I could ever ask of her. She did it, and I will always love her for it.

The next hardest thing that life brought me was being locked up in BDF, incarcerated for eighty-six days. I was trying for three years not to go, or didn't want anyone to find out, but since I was trying to get a good job so that I could take care of my family, the inevitable happened. It was discovered and I was locked up. I had never been in trouble with the law like that before. I was locked up when I was married to my first wife because she abused me, and when I got tired of it I retaliated, and was locked up for a few hours. She, her mom, and my mother came and bailed me out. I had to go to counseling, even though she should have gone. But that time of being locked up was just for a few hours, compared to eighty-six days.

Yes, I tried everything in my power not to end up there, but I did. But you know, through the grace of God I made it. I could have been hurt, or even killed, because of the crime I was in for, but I wasn't. Again, His grace. I had only one pair of underwear, but I made it through with His grace. I was basically alone, with no help or guidance. Cold, hard floor, hard bed, and nasty detention facility food. I didn't even have any visitors. That's what made it rough. Everyone around me was having visitors, had money for the commissary, had snacks, had clean underwear, and was being taken care of by someone on the outside, but not me. I was alone. The pastor didn't come see me, my wife was cheating on me with her ex-husband, and I was inside, not wanting to be there.

But through the grace of God, when the eighty-sixth day came, He said no more. I was released, went to trial, and was embarrassed as the charges were being read. I didn't have a choice but to be put on the registry because I couldn't get an attorney. I couldn't get out by talking to someone, or at least have someone at my back. So you see, being incarcerated for eighty-six days and losing my mom in less than seventeen years was a bit much, but through the grace of God, I made it. If you don't know me, you don't know what I've been through. You don't know my story, and you shouldn't judge me. Why? Because all have sinned and fallen short of the glory of God (Romans 3:23), and I made it.

Chapter Forty
LETTER TO CRICKET

Dear Cricket,

This letter has been a long time coming. It's been almost three years since we've communicated. It's been over three years since I've had the nerve to do this. You're all grown up now; you're nineteen years old, and all I can think of is how I allowed myself to be used to corrupt a sweet little girl that your mother gave birth to. This letter will tell you how I felt after the discovery of what I'd done to you.

You see, Cricket, sin is never a good feeling, and when we belong to God, He's not going to let it feel good. You were a sweet little girl when I first met you, and you didn't like me because I was dating your mother, and I didn't know how to take that. I've been around children my whole life and it was absurd for a child not to like me. I'd done everything possible to try to get you to like me. I was always racking my brains to see what I was doing wrong. It was to no avail. But when you were about to turn twelve, your mother and I worked together to give you a hotel birthday party, and it was as if I became a hero to you. You were truly surprised, and I will always remember that day. You practically jumped out of your clothes when everyone yelled, "Surprise!" I felt good; I felt as if I had done something great in your eyes. I was just trying to let you know that I truly cared about you, too, and not just your mom. But again, I really didn't know how to do it; I was a novice at this whole thing.

I let my aunt read this and she felt my pain through this whole thing. She told me, "You had no one in your early years to tell you some of the things you would be challenged with later in life. If you did, you would have known how to handle getting involved with women with children."

When I read that in an e-mail from her, I looked hard inside my heart and knew she was right. There was no manual with this thing. I was just trying to do everything right for you and your mother and brother. But my whole thinking when your mother and I got together was wrong. I was not being the role model I should have been, and I dropped the ball. I got caught up with my flesh and forgot about you and your brother. My flesh took control, and all my other thinking, all my knowledge of God, just left.

I've always prided myself on living for God and doing what was right, and when I fell to the flesh, I not only hurt you, I hurt God. When you hurt a child of God, there are consequences, and you were His child. You were very impressionable. When you started sitting close to me, and wanting to be with me and have "our time" at the end of the day, I didn't know what I was allowing myself to be set up for. We used to watch TV together and have quality time, and even fall asleep on the couch next to each other.

Even when we were getting ready for one of the church's banquets, you gave me flack when we were trying to take a family picture. You were a tough cookie, but that was fine. I just couldn't figure out what was going on at that time. I did think that we were getting some leeway when, at the end of a night of watching TV, you would kiss me on my cheek and say good night. I felt good. Or even driving you somewhere and dropping you off, and you'd give me a hug. I didn't think much of it.

But that evening, when the kisses began to turn to pecks on the lips, and then you started to touch me here and there once in a while, an alarm should have gone off. But I guess I was looking for acceptance from you, which was really wrong. I should have told your mother at that moment, so that she could have talked to you, but I didn't. I was trying to be a daddy to you, or so I thought, instead of a man taking care of you. And with sin, it starts off small and we think we have it under control, until we find out later that we really don't. You unknowingly figured out how to arouse me, and one thing led to another, and we ended up doing things that were inappropriate. I remember trying to talk to you about it, asking if you knew what would happen if we got caught. I guess that went in one ear and out the other. We even talked about you being jealous of your mother, and I asked why you were jealous of her.

I was been uncomfortable many times when your mother and I would be lying in bed and you'd want my attention, and you were even mad because I was with her. You see, at the time I didn't know I was between a rock and a hard place. I had a little girl who fell in love with me and a wife I was trying to be a husband to. I'd never thought that I'd ever be put in a situation like that, but it happened.

What I'm trying to say is that it wasn't your fault, it was all mine. I was the adult in this, and I shouldn't have been trying to please whatever awakened in you. I should have stopped it. You know how many times I tried, but couldn't because I got caught up in trying to keep you happy. But that, too, was wrong. There were times I wanted your mom to take you with her; I didn't want to be left with you because I was weak and didn't want to deal with you when you had the urges. It was safer for both of us if you weren't around me or I wasn't around you.

Cricket, I love you and I never wanted to hurt you. I wanted you to be able to grow up and find someone to love you for you, for your mind and your heart, not for your body. That's not love. I didn't do the right thing. I didn't protect you, not even from myself. This is something I'll never forget, something I'll always remember as a lesson for the rest of my life. I'm asking you to forgive me for dropping the ball, and not sticking to my promise of trying to fix this. This was only something that God could fix, and He had to do it His way because we couldn't do it.

You're all grown up now, driving, working, and living life. I hope one day, if we ever meet again, that you won't hate me for ruining your life. God has brought me a mighty long way. I just want you to be happy, and to know that in my heart you'll always be my little sweet Cricket.

Love,
Mr. Kai

Chapter Forty-One
PROBATION ENDING

The other day, as I was thinking about my probation ending, I realized another chapter in my life is about to end. For most of the past three years and eighty-six days, I've been in the system. I've had five probation officers; I had to report to them a various number of times throughout the week. I've had to change my work schedule for home visits, which is hard when you're trying to work at a job that God blessed you with. Did they care? I don't know, but it seemed like they didn't. My last probation officer made the last six months of my life very difficult. I've done everything she's asked me to do. Again, I've made arrangements to be home when I should have been working, and when it was down to the last day, I called her and she said she hadn't done a review of my case yet. Now mind you, this was three days before my case closed, and she was telling me this mess.

I was at work that day. I was angry, I was upset, and I wanted to cry, because I've done everything the system asked me to do, and I had a lazy probation officer that wouldn't do her job. I've basically had to keep track of her, to make sure she does what she's supposed to do. And I know the only thing she has to say is that she's not the one on probation, because I've heard her say that before. I cried that day at work, in secrecy. I have to stay in a good mood because people around me are looking to me to help them get through the day. But I'm thankful that I have a job, and a supervisor that knows I'm faithful, and one who is willing to work with me.

I thank God for my supervisor. She gets on my nerves at times, but deep down she's a sweetheart. She said she's willing to help me get through this and that is a blessing. It was only an act of God that, four months after being released from BDF, I was able to find gainful employment at my current job, and the Lord even elevated me months later. It was amazing. Eight months after my release I was receiving a favor from the Lord. December 17, 2012, will come, and my current probation officer will have to release me. She hasn't realized that I have God's favor upon my life, and she or the system can't do anything to me without God's approval.

Chapter Forty-Two
OBEDIENCE IS BETTER THAN SACRIFICE

I remember a time in BDF that I was learning what can and can't happen to you when you go before the judge, and also what your attorneys don't do for you. What stuck in my mind was hearing a young man say that he can't do probation because he messes up all the time and would get sent back to jail. I learned that if you get a ten-year sentence when you're sentenced, and your attorney gets you off with three to five years' probation, then you get back more years than what your sentence is.

When I heard that, I never thought I'd be going through it. But the attorney I had told me I was going to have to take the probation deal of three years and be on the registry, and I'd be set free. So, not really knowing what was going on because I'd had only five-minute discussions with him, I took it, due to the fact that I wanted to get out of a place I didn't want to be and was ready to go.

The main part of my probation was that I wasn't able to have any contact with the victim and I had to register with the Sex Offender Registry every sixth months at that time. But as time went on the laws changed, and I had to register every three months in order not to have to go back to jail. And for now, if I miss at any time, I will go back to jail.

So the Lord gave this to me when he said, "Obedience is better than sacrifice." For the first time in my life I had to be quiet, obey the rules, and be obedient—first to the law of God and then to the law of the land. I basically had to be quiet for three years and not say a word, or even be near my former stepdaughter. When God tells us not to do something, we're not to do it. But we live in a society that doesn't understand that. The word tells us how to live daily and yet we disobey it. The laws of driving tell us what to do and what not to do. We shouldn't speed, and yet we do; we shouldn't smoke, and yet we do; we shouldn't do this or that, and yet we do. We want to teach our children how to obey, and yet we're not obedient on our jobs.

Jesus says love as I have loved you (John 13:34, 15:9, 15:12), and we do sometimes. We also love when and how we want to love, when it's convenient to us—at times only then, if that.

This was a whole new experience for me because I had to do it. I didn't have a choice if I wanted to stay free until the probation was over. I thought about what that young man in BDF said. I made it through because I wanted to, and I didn't do it by myself, it was all with the help of God. I know I couldn't do it by myself. I asked my Creator to help me get back to where I had been and in three years He did it. He helped me learn how to rely on Him and not worry about all the things going on around me. In three years I've learned the real meaning of "obedience is better than sacrifice."

Chapter Forty-Three

BE NOT CONFORMED

"And be not conformed to this world: but be ye transformed by the renewing of your mind, that ye may prove what is that good, and acceptable, and perfect, will of God" (Romans 12:2, KJV). This is what the word says. This is my most recent thought; I'm a man that was raised in the church. I went to a Catholic Church for a part of my life. I've always studied the word, and gotten A's in it as well. I then started going to a Mennonite Church after I dedicated my life to Christ and got baptized the right way, submerged in water.

I then looked up the definition of conform and this is what it said: to comply with rules, standards, or laws. For the first time in my life, I understood what this verse meant. I did the total opposite when, at the age of twenty-five, I started complying with the standards of the world. As I said, I was in church my whole life, but Satan knew my weakness, which I thought I had under control. My entire life I'd never had a young lady take an interest in me to the point of going out and then having sex with me. So God allowed him to let one entice me enough that I started going out of my box. We have to be careful when we start going out of our box. The funny thing is that I met her in church. I've learned that every church girl isn't all the way saved. So, after meeting my first wife, soon afterward we started fornicating. I didn't even think about all the Bible studies I'd been to, or being a Sunday school teacher. I just started complying with the world's way of doing things, because that was the one thing Satan knew he could get me with.

As I said in an earlier chapter, we didn't become friends, we didn't really get to know each other, I got caught up in the wrong part of the relationship, and I thought that by doing that, I was in love with her, and she was in love with me. On the contrary, we didn't know each other at all, and when things started falling apart the real her came out. She started beating me when she got angry. I knew then that something was wrong. I can reflect on it now because I've grown, been sanctified by God, and look at things in a whole new perspective. When I conformed to the ways of my flesh and the world by fornicating, I was not able to focus on what God had planned for me. I kept trying to fit a circle into a square, and we know that really doesn't work.

Then, after the first marriage fell apart, I had the nerve to do it again. I met a variety of women online, then had a girlfriend, fornicated, and thought I was in love again. Then this crazy musician church man, who had one foot in and one foot out, met another church girl, fornicated, and then married her. Yes, I thought I was doing right by conforming again.

Now, twenty-four years later, I understand what that verse means. After I was incarcerated for eighty-six days, the Lord renewed my mind and gave me a new life. He gave me a calling. He needed me to be still and know that He is God. He needed me to study His word; He needed me to be alone with Him so that He could talk to me. He needed me not focus on those women, the church, or the mess I was in, but to give Him my full attention. The renewing of the mind takes time. It's not an overnight process, it's a me-and-God time where He can saturate my mind with His word. I'm a completely different person now. I look at things from a spiritual viewpoint. I don't look at things as the world does or the way my flesh views them, because I'm no longer conforming to the patterns of this world or my flesh. I'm conformed to the ways of God, and I thank Him for saving me from myself.

Chapter Forty-Four

SIFTED AS WHEAT, LUKE 22:31-32

As I'm nearing the end of this first book, the Lord led me today to hear a song titled "Say A Prayer." As I listened to it, the songwriter quoted what Jesus said in (Luke 22:31-32, NIV): "Simon, Simon, Satan has asked to sift you as wheat. But I have prayed for you, Simon, that your faith may not fail. And when you have turned back, strengthen your brothers." In this, Jesus was telling Peter that Satan wants to separate you from me as a farmer separates wheat from husks. Satan desired to have Peter in his hands instead of in Jesus's hands. But Jesus told Peter that He would be praying for him, that his faith would not fail. And when you come out of what Satan is trying to do, you will have a job to strengthen others that will go through trials also.

Jesus said this because He knew Peter had to go through the test, just as He went through His test in the wilderness. After forty days and forty nights of fasting and praying, Satan came to Him and tried to test Him and break His will. But Jesus used scripture on Satan and he had to back off. Peter thought he was ready to go with Jesus anywhere, and he was—until the test.

I cried when I heard that song this morning, because of the line: "Like you did for Peter, say a prayer for me." Why am I saying this? Well, God gave me this epiphany. Satan peeked into my future over twenty-three years ago and saw something that he didn't want to happen. He saw the true man of God that I would become. So what did he do? He did all he could to keep me from getting here. He didn't want Kai to reach this point in his life. A point where my faith is stronger than it's ever been. Christ was interceding for me the whole time and I didn't even realize it.

Through all the storms, winds, trials, and struggles, I won. He didn't think I would make it being incarcerated for eighty-six days, but I did. He didn't think I would make it when I lost everything, but I did. He didn't think I would make it when I was put out of my church, but I made it through that, too. You see, Jesus and the Holy Spirit refused to give up on me because I still have work to do for my Heavenly Father.

Yes, I was sifted, left for dead, separated from everything that I love—my family, my God, and my friends. But that wasn't the end, truly it wasn't. It was just the beginning of what Kai will become for the rest of his life: a man that truly loves God and God's people, and was shown how to show love to everyone. Why? Because Jesus, the Holy Spirit, and his Father in Heaven never gave up on him.

Epilogue

LETTER TO MR. MONTGOMERY

Dear Mr. Montgomery,

I'm writing this letter to encourage you to continue in His name. You've been through some difficult times in the past twenty-three years of your life. If you look at it, that's basically half your lifetime. You've fallen into circumstances allowed by God because of your own desire and passion for things that looked good but really weren't. That wasn't the way you were raised, but like many people in the world, you got caught up. You tried to be the good and perfect Christian, and I remember you getting burned out at your church in Philadelphia when trying to take on so many responsibilities—to the point that you got tired and were hoping others would come along and help out so that you'd have some relief.

God knew your weaknesses. He knew you'd never been on a real date. He knew that if He allowed Satan to put the right person in your life and pull the right strings, you'd take the bait. He allowed you to let yourself be played like a fiddle. God allowed the accuser to pull you out of your comfort zone by presenting the right young lady—a church girl, at that—to bring you out of the morals that you were raised in. You see, you couldn't handle the freedom when she said yes and wanted to lay with you: your first sexual experience at the age of twenty-five. Then you thought that was love, and it was only lust. Love was what you wanted, what you needed. So what did you do? You married her, not really knowing her or even giving yourself time to get to know her. And what happened in the end? It was a debacle. It ended, and you ended up alone and in bankruptcy court.

And let's not forget that in all this mess, your mother, who you loved so much, died of cancer when you really needed her. I admit I didn't think you were going to make it through that one. You're always calm, cool, and collected, but that almost took a toll on you. And again, you got caught up on the Internet and found a new love, Internet love. Yes, Satan was truly seeking to destroy you, and God allowed it to happen so that you would go back to Him, your first love. When Pandora's box was opened it was hard for you to try to close it yourself.

You were having too much fun, one foot in the church and one foot out, so why close it? So what did God allow him to do? He allowed him to bring another one into your life, and you did the same thing again. Fornicated while saying it was love and moved to Baltimore. Yes, it was becoming a pattern, but you couldn't see it. You were "in love," and how many of us know that that was a lie?

So when that relationship was over, and you were tired, what happened? Well, we already know. You did it again. Just after you receive the divorce papers from your first wife, you go and marry again for lust and sex. Can you even tell me what was on your mind, man? Can you even tell me why you didn't give yourself a break to get your head on right? You were jumping right from the pot into the kettle and on a road to destruction. You never gave yourself time to get to know these women that were soon to be your demise. They never knew you and you never knew them; they were just sex and lust, and your crazy behind thought it was love and you married them. And what happened with each wife? You ended up divorced and in bankruptcy court.

Then I find out that in the second marriage you were incarcerated for eighty-six days for hurting a child. Now, I know you, and I know that is not you. Something had to happen to make you not think before it all happened. Mr. Kai, you've been working with children your whole life, and I know you would never hurt a child. I know you would die for a child if need be. So something had to happen for you to do this. I don't care what others say, I know you. So whatever happened, I know you weren't thinking, and the tricks of the accuser approved by God got you trapped, and unfortunately a little child was your undoing.

But you know what the word says, "All have sinned and fallen short of the glory of God" (Romans 3:23). I know that was a hard fall for you. I know you didn't really want to hurt that child; I know you wouldn't hurt anyone. But God had big plans for you and the accuser thought he could ruin and stop those plans, not knowing that those same plans were to bring you closer to Him. I heard that while you were in BDF, you received your calling from God. God was after you your whole life, but you were so worried about trying to get a date, trying to get a woman to like you, that you weren't listening, and when the first thing came along that would pay you some attention, you took the bait. But God, who's so merciful, wasn't going to let you fall without being there to pick you up. When others turned their backs on you, and I heard all about it, He wasn't going to.

You have dreams that God said you would fulfill. You had to learn how to forgive yourself for hurting that child, and I know that was the hardest thing for you to do, because I know you. You're a child of the Creator, and when you fell our Heavenly Father was waiting for you to come to Him, to allow Him to wipe you off so that you could keep moving. You're a new creature. The old is gone and the new has come, and if anyone, Mr. Kai, has anything to say, just tell them that you cried your last tear. God has forgiven you, and now you can look in the mirror and walk away, never forgetting what you look like because you're walking in His light.

Sincerely yours,
Mr. Hezekiah L. Montgomery

www.ingramcontent.com/pod-product-compliance
Lightning Source LLC
Chambersburg PA
CBHW070609300426
44113CB00010B/1476